Essential Wisdom for Leaders of Every Generation is not something you can read and digest in one sitting. Every section, every chapter, is to be taken in thoughtfully so it can be applied practically. Because what Randy Hain has put together here is as practical as it is truly essential. Give this book to those you care about who are or may one day be leaders. And keep a copy on your bedside table or in a handy place for your own regular boosts of incremental wisdom. This is a gem.

—**Patrick Lencioni**, *New York Times* Bestselling
Author and President, The Table Group

Essential Wisdom isn't a book; it is the mentor we all need to keep us focused on what really matters in leadership. The advice is simple and direct. It is practical and compelling. Don't just read this book; study this book, and you will not just become a better leader . . . you will become a better person. That is a promise!

—**Chester Elton**, The Apostle of Appreciation
and *New York Times* Bestselling Author,
Leading with Gratitude and *Anxiety at Work*

Randy Hain is one of the most authentic, optimistic, joyful, and giving people I know. Randy is a mentor and someone I turn to when I am seeking advice on career, family, and community issues. This book is for anyone who is seeking practical insights and wisdom in their everyday lives. I highly recommend *Essential Wisdom for Leaders of Every Generation!*

—**Jo Ann Herold**, Chief Marketing Officer,
The Honey Baked Ham Company

In his new book, *Essential Wisdom for Leaders of Every Generation*, Randy Hain shares a practical guide for leaders to navigate through the complexities of today's business environment in a thoughtful and practical manner that makes the reader reflect on ways to improve the way they connect and engage with people, how they build relationships and support their teams, and the importance of clear and concise communications. This guide helps leaders understand the fundamentals of leadership, the importance of being present, the mechanics of positively impacting others, and what leaders leave behind when it is all done. Randy's strong experience as a business professional and executive coach, combined with his sincere, practical, and faith-based style, make his book a must-read for leaders in all industries and of all ages.

—**Juan Perez**, CIO, UPS

Randy Hain continues to inspire, and this time he has created a personal and professional masterpiece to help guide not only the career professional, but also the working parent and the aspiring college student looking to start a career and wondering where and how to start. This book captures the essence of life leadership by highlighting the importance of character, authenticity, credibility, and maximizing efficiently in the workplace to allow for a more rewarding life. Randy's passion as an executive coach comes shining through as he challenges readers to be their best selves.

—**Misty Brown**, Southeastern Conference, Assistant Commissioner of Competition and Student-Athlete Engagement

The writer of Proverbs encourages us that "Wisdom is the principal thing; therefore, get wisdom: and with all thy getting, get understanding." Randy Hain offers leaders in every stage of their career an opportunity to gain wisdom from his decades of experience. He has spent his entire career helping people succeed in their careers and in life and now he has bundled his advice and wisdom into one volume in his new book, *Essential Wisdom for Leaders of Every Generation*. Read this fantastic book to help you gain wisdom and then apply it to gain understanding.

—**Dee Ann Turner**, Bestselling Author, *Bet on Talent and Crush Your Career*, CEO, Dee Ann Turner & Associates

Essential Wisdom for Leaders of Every Generation is not just a book about wisdom and leadership. It's a book about life, and how to approach it successfully. Leadership and life are about one thing: Relationships. Our relationship with ourselves as well as with others. There is so much valuable, concise, and practical wisdom in this book that you will want to carry it around with you all the time. I've known Randy Hain for decades, and it has been his personal mission to share as much of the wisdom that he has gained over his life as he can. He shares it willingly, with empathy, and with passion. This is a must-read.

    —Ray V. Padrón, CEO, Brightworth Private Wealth

Chock-full of excellent advice, *Essential Wisdom* is a masterful combination of practical guidance and tips that provide a roadmap to success and fulfillment. Randy Hain has remarkably condensed over two and a half decades of executive experience into one book designed to help you live your best life. Use this book as your GPS—to help you reach the destination you've always desired!

    —Virginia Means, Chief People Officer, United Distributors, Inc.

In his book *Essential Wisdom*, Randy Hain has done it again. He tackles significant topics we all face each day, and offers common sense, insights, and wisdom to those of us who may need a guide or a reminder. This book is full of actionable steps for anyone who is busy and needs to return to a solid foundation. This book provides a brain to pick and a kick in the seat of the pants. I recommend it to anyone.

    —Tim Elmore, Author and Founder, GrowingLeaders.com

Whether you are a young professional or a seasoned leader, *Essential Wisdom* is a practical guide to becoming an ideal teammate, an inspiring leader, and an overall better human being. Insightful, profound, and easy to apply, this book is a must-read!

    —Brandon Smith, Author, Educator, Executive Coach,
     and Host of *The Workplace Therapist Show* podcast

Randy Hain is an authentic and well-respected coach and mentor to many, including me for more than two decades. In his new book *Essential Wisdom for Leaders of Every Generation,* Randy describes the criticality of authenticity in leaders sharing their true selves, explaining it is not enough to simply be authentic but to also help others thrive in their own authenticity. This leadership characteristic is perhaps the most challenging among leaders, yet Randy explains how authenticity is the "gateway" to encourage others to bring their full and best selves to work.

—**Karen Bennett**, EVP and Chief People Officer, Cox Communications

Randy so simply yet powerfully reminds us that wisdom comes from the priorities we set and the choices we make . . . no matter our stage of life. The values and guiding principles of Faith, Family, and Work (in that order) as Randy says in the book, "serve as our inner voice to advise us about what is right or wrong." If we choose to put Faith and Family first, we will become truly authentic, credible, trustworthy, and irreplaceable leaders/contributors at work. Surround yourself with role models like Randy that will help you choose wisely. . . by so doing, you will become a role model of wisdom and success for generations to come."

—**Steve Hayes**, Believer, Husband, Father, Grandfather, and Senior Managing Director, Gallagher Executive Search and Leadership Advisors

As a young professional who is about to begin his career, *Essential Wisdom* offered me practical advice as I look to make an impact both at work and home and lead in a value-oriented way. Mr. Hain's insights on everything from moral living to time management, which are drawn from years of firsthand experience, have allowed me to see a preview of what lies ahead in my career and have given me steps to live my beliefs in a positive, healthy manner. Each chapter is structured to highlight practical applications for each lesson, which are very helpful for readers looking to take actionable steps to improve themselves. I would recommend this book to anyone who is graduating college and is looking to have a fulfilling, prosperous career.

—**Ben Lange,** Student, Brock School
of Business at Samford University

In the twenty years since we met, Randy has had a profound influence on my life. *Essential Wisdom* offers many of the same insights and practical ideas he has shared with me over the years. Thoughtfully reading his book will help you along the path toward becoming your true and best self and creating your legacy. I strongly recommend his book!

—**Dr. Ron Young**, Psychologist and Executive Coach, Trove, Inc.,
Founder and Chairman of the Board

Approachable. Honest. Candid. Respectful. Refreshing. A real friend. A real professional. If you know Randy Hain or have had the pleasure of meeting him, even if only briefly, you know this all to be true—and this book is an absolute mirror of his life, his work, his way. This is a must-read book if you are seeking an actionable path to a pragmatic, thoughtful, and practical approach on becoming a better "you," a better person, a better leader.

—**Michael Mathews**, SVP and CIO for Deluxe

There is a reason why Randy Hain keeps getting invited to speak to my students in the Brock School of Business at Samford University—his lectures are always marked by notable and actionable wisdom and are spot-on for the current generation. His new book, *Essential Wisdom for Leaders of Every Generation*, is more of the same and oozes Solomonic wisdom on every page. If you have ever wished someone would write a book that shows you how to apply the rich knowledge found in the book of Proverbs to the modern-day business world, your wish has come true!

—**Darin W. White, PhD,** Chair, Entrepreneurship, Management,
Marketing Department, Brock School
of Business, and Executive Director, Samford
University Center for Sports Analytics

It's easy to write about leadership, but it's hard to live what you write. Randy Hain truly is the kind of person he encourages us all to become—transparent, humble, committed, and incredibly generous. I have enjoyed Randy's writing for years. His work is easy and engaging to read, but you also feel that you're sitting with a wise mentor who is sharing his soul and helping you grow.

Essential Wisdom is a compilation of not only his recent thinking, but also his years of experience in the business world. This is not a book you read and then close the cover. It's a book you can go back to when you need inspiration and help. Randy encourages us in this book to use the workplace to make a difference in the lives of others and as a place for growing ourselves, and he shares the mindsets and the tools he himself uses to grow—like being authentic in a way that honors the authenticity of others, practicing "radical prioritization," and "living life in real time." Buy it, read it, and reread it.

—**Carolyn (Lyn) Turknett**, Co-founder,
Turknett Leadership Group

Randy Hain has hit it out of the park—again! This book is brimming with practical wisdom and ideas that will change your career. . . and your life. Randy's writing reflects his unique blend of experience, humility, and servant leadership to deliver a powerful, transformative message. Read this book, highlight it, reflect on it, and repeat. You'll be eternally grateful for the light Randy shines on your path.

—**Kevin Lowry,** CFO, RevLocal, LLC

Randy Hain has hit the mark with *Essential Wisdom*. I define *wisdom* as "a collection of experiences," and Randy is highly qualified to author a book about wisdom based on his successful track record as a leader, executive coach, consultant, and author. Additionally, having worked with Randy as my own executive coach, I can personally attest that Randy's leadership advice is both effective and results-oriented. Randy's thoughts on topics such as integrity, authenticity, candor, and balance are clear and concise. His guidance is both logical and executable. In this book, Randy has laid out a practical guide to developing yourself as a leader. I am confident that by employing the ideas offered here you will not only improve your own leadership abilities, but you will also enhance the lives of the people around you. *Essential Wisdom* is a must-read for anyone looking to take their leadership (and relationships) to the next level.

—**Craig A. Gunckel**, CEO of Iconex

Words like *authenticity, thoughtfulness, gratitude,* and *clarity* are often mistaken as *soft* skills in the marketplace. *Essential Wisdom* is packed with relatable stories and actionable next steps grounded in Randy Hain's signature style of teaching the HARD skills needed in the world today. This book is a must-read for anyone who is committed to growing and expanding their leadership skills and influence at work and at home in a meaningful way. *Essential Wisdom* is a perfect field guide to use throughout the year, and I always have it within arm's reach.

—**Ash Merchant**, President and CEO, Lionheart Partners

We often struggle with bringing our entire selves into our professional world for fear of relevance or causing unintended offense. Furthermore, we are constantly asked to replace our own judgment and experiences with superficial analysis of uncontextualized data. In this book, Randy helps us take a step back, embrace what matters in our lives, be true to ourselves, and redirect our professional course toward living more meaningful and fulfilling lives. Randy also reminds us that we must take back control of our schedules and focus on the quality of our moments versus their quantity. Finally, he reassures us that the friendships and relationships we've built over time are there to both help us and receive our help if we include one another in our process for defining, executing, and achieving our life goals. This book is a great read for professionals at all stages, whether you are preparing to enter the workforce (finishing college), just starting your first job, or even if you are a seasoned executive who is looking to regain balance and meaning to your own life journey.

—**Ricardo Alvarado**, Director, Jabian Consulting

Essential Wisdom for Leaders is a book that you will keep on your desk and refer to over and over again. Every chapter is a unique, practical lesson for navigating your leadership journey. Not only will it guide you personally, it's also the playbook you will gladly teach and pass

down to the future leaders on your team. Congratulations to Randy Hain for wrapping his experiences into a book we can all learn from!
—**Terrence McCrossan,** President and CEO, Oversight

Essential Wisdom provides a fresh, thoughtful, and authentic perspective on leadership and life. Randy reveals his lived experience throughout the lessons, providing a practical guidebook for developing leadership and relationship skills regardless of your current situation. The essays in the book, based on Randy's decades of experience leading people, building teams, and raising a family, are the kind of essays you can read multiple times, gaining new insights with each read. Following the recommendations and guides Randy includes likely will propel your career and improve your leadership effectiveness.
—**Amelia Fox,** Chief Strategy Officer for Lutheran Services Florida

Randy Hain provides a treasure of wisdom in his latest book. Always the sage mentor, Hain weaves a compelling narrative, mixing genuine knowledge with concrete advice. The melding of the theoretical with the practical, Hain's signature style, allows readers to understand and to engage crucial issues for creating lives rich in meaning, gratitude, and mission. This book will resonate with a wide audience, and I enthusiastically recommend this book equally for high school students and seasoned business executives, for the newly employed and those nearing retirement.
—**Paul J. Voss, PhD,** President, Ethikos, and
Associate Professor, Georgia State University

Essential Wisdom for Leaders of Every Generation provides a wealth of practical, surprisingly easy-to-adopt tactics and leadership lessons for those who are just starting their career journey—and those of us who are "well-traveled" professionals. As a friend and colleague, I've watched Randy practice these fundamental concepts for many years with his coaching clients, developing stronger, more connected, and authentic leaders at every level. Randy's courageous and candid feedback, RAPKG, and commitment to our business relationship have made a pivotal difference in my own career and have accelerated the growth of countless up-and-coming leaders on my team. His advice is quite simply career-changing.

> —**Mary Ellen Marcilliat-Falkner,** Executive Vice President and Chief People Officer, Cox Media Group

Randy Hain has been a longtime go-to source for leaders seeking wisdom to become better leaders. *Essential Wisdom* is the culmination of a lifetime of leadership and experience that Randy has exemplified. This is a book you will act on, not just a book you will read. The proven concepts that Randy shares are ones you'll embrace to advance your life's work. Thank you, Randy, for producing this impactful work and helping us all thrive on the leadership journey!

> —**Tom Darrow, SHRM-SCP,** Founder and Principal, Talent Connections, LLC and Career Spa, LLC

It is my great blessing to call Randy Hain my friend. As I read his words, I hear an authentic voice who brings his values to life every day. He deftly links the responsibility of leaders to fulfilling a purpose that extends before self into relationship with others all in the service of God. Please read and reflect on the messages shared in these pages if you want to fully lead to help others grow.

> —**Patricia Falotico,** VP, Client Development Pathbuilders, Former CEO, The Robert K. Greenleaf Center for Servant Leadership

Randy Hain is widely known as a highly successful and well-connected business leader, executive coach, and mentor. His many books on leadership, faith, and life have been inspirational and impactful. His latest offering, *Essential Wisdom for Leaders of Every Generation*, deserves to be considered among the most helpful of leadership books. Randy draws on a lifetime of wisdom gained from his professional experiences, his Catholic faith that guides his direction and choices, and the timeless lessons learned from wise and loving parents. *Essential Wisdom* identifies and connects these important leadership ideas and best practices to relevant and actionable guidance that will make a difference in your professional (and personal) life. I believe that now, more than ever, successful leaders require this essential wisdom.

—**Michael Bickerstaff**, President, Virtue@Work

With *Essential Wisdom for Leaders of Every Generation*, Randy Hain utilizes his vast career experiences to unlock keys for today's leaders as well as those aspiring to lead thriving organizations. The author speaks to the reader in impactful and meaningful ways through the lens of a talented, successful servant leader. This book provides leadership truths that, if adhered to, will produce great fruit in our organizations. In this book, Randy Hain has been able achieve that rare feat: provide readers of all generations with tangible, useful insights into the complexities of leading others.

—**Charles M. Carson, PhD**, Dean and Professor, Management, Brock School of Business at Samford University

Essential Wisdom offers compelling essential truths that all leaders should subscribe to. It is one of the very best books on leadership. What I like most about the book is that the lessons that are taught are from Randy's practical experiences as a leader himself, or from observations as an executive coach, mentor, or advisor. Randy offers readers the opportunity to evaluate themselves personally as a leader and provides a pragmatic guide on how to build their leadership muscle and gain self-mastery. Whether you're an aspiring leader, new to a leadership role, or a seasoned executive, leaders at all levels can find value in this work.

—**Willie Mazyck**, Senior Vice President, Talent Development, XPO Logistics

A constant challenge for busy leaders is discerning which voice one chooses to listen to from a cacophony proposing advice. Randy Hain has become an indispensable voice for me. In the aptly titled *Essential Wisdom*, Randy has compiled a veritable treasure chest of sage, practical insights. Randy possesses a remarkable ability to blend his deep experience with timeless, principle-based, and faith-filled guidance, culminating into simple yet powerful action steps. His voice is an essential clarion call for leaders, reminding us just how to do right things, and to do things right. I am delighted to add this extraordinary compilation to my ready-reference shelf and offer *Essential Wisdom* my highest recommendation to leaders.

—**Doran N. Oancia**, CEO, Chemex Global, Inc.

Randy Hain continues to provide practical leadership insights from his life experience. His authenticity comes across in sharing the challenges and opportunities of living his moral compass. Spending the time to define our values that act as the forces to energize our compass allows us to live a strong, impactful, entire human life, in real time! These principles are excellent for all of us given the challenging aspects of our world today.

—**Joe George,** President, Cox Automotive Mobility

Randy Hain is one of those rare individuals whose strength of character and commitment to authenticity make him humble, approachable, and real as a leader, coach, mentor, and friend. *Essential Wisdom for Leaders of Every Generation* is a way of "sitting down with Randy over coffee," where he offers guidance that is perfectly timed as we navigate an uncertain journey. His own lessons learned from a well-examined life are presented in a no-nonsense, practical manner yet with a keen understanding of the struggle to stay true to one's values and ideals in the workplace and in society today. The wisdom Randy generously offers leaders transcends age, experience, and culture, and addresses the heart of leadership— staying aligned with who you are, regardless of the role you play.

—**Andrea Chilcote**, Executive Coach and
President, Morningstar Ventures Inc.

Randy Hain's newest book, *Essential Wisdom for Leaders of Every Generation,* is a true "how-to" for anyone needing a refresher or just getting into the world of business. The advice and expertise he offers is the same he would offer anyone in a face-to-face conversation. The step-by-step instruction goes into detail as to what can be done to thrive in the world of business. The tips and tricks within this book have allowed me to jump-start my career.

—**Bain McCullough**, Young Professional

My friend Randy Hain has written an authentic guidebook for leaders and aspiring leaders who want to be more effective in their role and become a shining example for those around them. Randy's extensive career as a senior business leader, leadership consultant, executive coach, and man of faith has equipped him with the experience and insight to be an expert on this subject. *Essential Wisdom* is based on the foundational need for a moral compass and illustrates ways to build—and more importantly, use—that moral compass over time. He adds to this foundation the practice of authenticity, the importance of credibility, and the gift of being present or living life in real time. This book is packed with wisdom and should be required reading for all leaders.

—**David V. McAnally Jr.**, Vice President,
Sales Training/Partner, LocumTenens.com

Randy Hain is a wellspring of wisdom whose actions match his words. We need more people like Randy in our world today for many reasons, starting with his humility and integrity. This book is yet another example of Randy's unflinching commitment to pour into others. Like many, I am blessed to call Randy a friend.

—**Glen Jackson**, Co-Founder, Jackson Spalding

ESSENTIAL WISDOM
for Leaders of Every Generation

Randy Hain

SERVIAM PRESS

ISBN: 978-1-7377244-0-7 (softcover)
ISBN: 978-1-7377244-1-4 (e-book)

Published by Serviam Press, LLC
www.serviampress.com

This book is dedicated to:

Steve and Sandi Hain

*I am truly grateful for your love,
encouragement, and gifts of wisdom.*

CONTENTS

PART FOUR: WHAT'S IT ALL FOR?

Introduction

Wisdom is not a product of schooling,
but of the lifelong attempt to acquire it.

ALBERT EINSTEIN

Essential Wisdom is unlike the other books I have written. The content is largely drawn from articles and blog posts I have written over the last decade through my lens as an executive coach, leadership consultant, husband, father, and community servant. There is also plenty of fresh writing mixed in for good measure. Before I was an executive coach and consultant, I spent twenty-five years in executive roles, including senior operations leadership for a national retailer, vice-president of people for a $2 billion national restaurant company, and later as the managing partner of a well-respected national executive recruiting firm.

My goal with *Essential Wisdom* is not to offer another tired book on leadership to occupy space on your bookshelf, but instead offer you a helpful guidebook filled with insights, ideas, and best practices I believe all leaders should think about and do well in order to be more effective in their roles. Leaders and aspiring leaders of every age and any stage of their career journey will hopefully find practical nuggets of wisdom they can use in their daily lives.

When you review the table of contents, you will see the broad spectrum of topics in this book ranging from discerning your *moral compass* to *practicing candor* to better *time management* to defining the *legacy* you will leave behind. The lessons in this book are drawn from decades of life and work experiences and observations from my coaching and consulting work with leaders across the globe. I strive to be authentic in everything I do, and so you will read in sporadic places throughout this book a few references to prayer or the positive influence of my Catholic faith. I have always believed in consistently showing up as the same person at work as I do at home, at church, or with my friends. Every day I work with professionals who have different beliefs and opinions from mine, and I appreciate the diversity of thoughts, backgrounds, and experiences this brings into my life. I am also grateful for the mutual respect and civility, regardless of differences in belief or backgrounds, that have been the hallmarks of the relationships I have built over my career.

This book is dedicated to my parents, Steve and Sandi Hain. My mother passed away over a decade ago, and we are blessed to still have my father with us. They set a wonderful example as parents and always worked hard to provide for our family. I will never forget the important life discussions at the dinner table, the quality time they invested in me and my sister, and the remarkable consistency with which they did their best to do the right thing every day. They set a timeless example for me when I was growing up that we need to see more of in today's world:

- They modeled a phenomenal work ethic.
- They lived with their values front and center.
- They quietly but purposefully committed themselves to serving others at work, in their church, and in the community.
- Their priorities were God, family, and work . . . in that order.
- They never failed to pass along the wisdom and practical lessons from their life experiences to me and my sister and others who knew them.

I will be forever grateful for the lessons they taught me in my time on this earth, which I continue to pass along as I reflect on the example of their lives or receive wise counsel from my dad. This book is my own small effort to share those lessons with my children, future grandchildren, and other wisdom seekers I encounter in my life.

I truly hope you find this work to be helpful and valuable.

PART ONE

Embracing the Fundamentals

CHAPTER 1

The Need for a Moral Compass

We are in the middle of a profound sea of change affecting all aspects of life: social, cultural, economic, and political. Changes are being played out all over the world. Prompted by the alienation and uncertainty of our age, people—now more than ever—want to find a reliable moral compass. They want to integrate their whole selves; integrate who they are with what they do. Some are coming to recognize a deep-seated drive within each one of us to use our talents, intelligence and imagination for the greater good.

From a Talk Given by the Late James L. Nolan,
Author of *Doing the Right Thing at Work*

Almost every company has a values statement, but rarely can the typical employee recite it—or even articulate the ways the company practices them. Values should be more than a plaque on a wall or a bulleted list on a website. They are guiding principles and serve as our inner voice to advise us about what is right or wrong. It is important that personal and professional values are integrated and aligned. A finely tuned moral compass can provide us with a set of core values that help guide our decisions throughout our lives. Ideally, there should be a balance between what is good for us and what is good for our company (and society in general).

Leaders are not likely to begin their careers with a fully developed moral compass. Good moral and ethical judgment is learned and cultivated over the course of a career. Over time, a person's moral compass will likely evolve based on some combination of faith, life experiences, relationships, and the simple passage of time. Leaders with a strong moral compass will work hard to live up to their values and make sure the colleagues and clients in their circle of influence will always feel the positive impact of those values. My moral compass has largely been determined by how I was raised by my parents, my life and work experiences, the crucible of adversity, helpful mentors, friends who challenge me, and my strong faith. How about you?

The most important aspect of having a moral compass is actually *using* that moral compass. If we invest in developing a moral compass and then ignore what it tells us or never read it at all, I hope we can agree it does us absolutely no good. By "reading" our moral compass, I simply mean thoughtfully and logically considering our choices in a given situation and making sure our internal values and ethics square up with the decisions we make. Are they well aligned or are they in conflict?

With leadership comes not only rights and privileges, but also duties and obligations. I am making the basic assumption that if you're reading this book, you desire to accept these duties and obligations and to be leaders of strong character who strive to do the right thing at work and serve the greater good, as my dear friend and mentor Jim Nolan described in the quote at the top of the page. Many of us are tired of the division, confusion, and anger so prevalent in society today and want to make a positive difference in the world (and in the workplace). If so, how do we continue to refine, develop, and use our moral compass? How do we apply these positive behaviors?

Six Ideas for Effectively Using Your Moral Compass

1. **Do you have the right list?** Clarify your core values. Write a list of what they are, then modify your behavior to work with your values rather than against them. Distinguish between your *aspirational* values and your *actual* values. In other words, there are values you truly live day in and day out and other values you aspire to achieve but have yet to act on. I recommend that your list of actual core values be five or fewer.

2. **Ask the right questions**. To find out if the core values you have selected are ones you actually live and act on, ask yourself the following questions:
   - Are you willing to *fight* for them?
   - Are you willing to *sacrifice* for them?
   - Are you willing to *spend time* on them?
   - Are you willing to *share* them publicly with others?

   By wrestling with and eventually answering these questions, you can begin the journey of discovering what really matters to you, aligning your actions with your core values, and raising your expectations for how business can be a positive force in our society.

3. **Navigate the challenges.** There will often be stress and negative pressure associated with situations and encounters where you need to rely on your moral compass and make the right decisions. It can feel like

a shock to the system if you are not prepared. The capacity to manage these challenges will be critical to your long-term success in living out your values in the workplace.

4. **Resist excuses.** "Everybody else is doing it." "It's not my responsibility." "It's not that big of a deal, and we should let it go this time." "I am afraid of the ramifications if I speak up." When you ignore your moral compass and hide your values in the face of challenging ethical situations, you are making harmful compromises that eat away at you and diminish your overall leadership. Resist this temptation. Take a stand.

5. **Keep it simple.** The mere idea of engaging your moral compass may invoke perceptions of a standard that is almost impossible to achieve. Far from it! Consider focusing on the small acts of good, ethical, and moral behavior that can help you make good use of your moral compass and develop them at the same time. *Treat others well. Honor your commitments. Don't lie or mislead. Give proper credit where it is deserved. Practice servant leadership inside your company and in your community. Own your mistakes. Be humble.* These behaviors are basic yet powerful, and all of us are capable of exhibiting them each day. These behaviors can also serve as a supportive foundation to help you make the more difficult choices that will inevitably come your way throughout your career.

6. **Be consistent and courageous.** Like it or not, fully utilizing the moral compass you have carefully worked hard to build requires you to be a consistent role model.

You can't ask others to follow an ethical and moral path in the workplace with certain expected behaviors if you are not willing to consistently do the same. That would be the worst form of hypocrisy. Be prepared at times to walk a lonely road. It takes courage to realize that you may sometimes be the *only* person willing to take a stand and do the right thing . . . and do it anyway.

I hope these six ideas will appropriately frame your thinking about ways to fully engage your moral compass. Utilizing your moral compass is important, but so is developing approaches to *strengthen* it. How do you strengthen your moral compass? Where can you go for help and encouragement?

Four Ideas for Strengthening Your Moral Compass

1. **Seek out good mentors and role models**. Whom do you know who has a strong moral compass? Who models the right behaviors you wish to emulate? Whom can you turn to for answers to your difficult ethical or moral questions? Reflect carefully about your current work colleagues or professionals outside of your company who may be willing to spend time with you in a mentoring capacity. This can also include family and close friends. Always be clear about what you are seeking from them and be respectful of their time. I have greatly benefited from these types of mentors over the course of my career, and I would have had a significantly more difficult path without their help.

2. **Choose friends who will challenge you to grow.** "Iron sharpens iron and men sharpen men," as the old

saying goes. Choose your friends well. Spend quality time with people who will challenge you to grow your moral compass. For example, I am part of a Catholic men's group that I helped co-found in 2007. We are all businesspeople seeking practical ways to integrate our faith with our work. These good men are a great source of personal and spiritual growth for me, and I am grateful for their friendship and willingness to always challenge me to be a better father, husband, and business leader.

3. **Choose your environment wisely**. Sometimes you just don't fit a team or organization. You may have a feeling in the pit of your stomach that says you should just walk away because their values directly conflict with yours. Listen to that inner voice. If interviewing for a job, ask probing questions of the interviewer to get a feeling for their moral compass and the values of their organization. We all have to make a living, but we should never have to compromise our values or who we are to do so.

4. **Find a strong pillar to lean on.** The greatest source for clearly understanding what doing the right thing at work and in life looks like comes from my Catholic faith. My greatest source of strength comes from my active prayer life. My moral compass would be greatly diminished if it was not fed daily by my life as a Christian. This is my example, but I know countless other professional men and women of all ages and backgrounds who would share similar views about their Christian, Jewish, Buddhist, Muslim, or other faith

experiences. I am *not* saying people without faith are missing a moral compass. No, not at all! As long as your source of inspiration provides you with an *unchanging standard*, you're starting in the right place. It's unlikely that any two moral compasses are exactly alike, but most share common traits that can help you distinguish right from wrong.

A well-formed moral compass can help us strike the right balance in our lives between emotion and reason, idealism and practicality, and our needs and those of others. Simply put, a moral compass can and should guide us toward what we *ought* to do in a given situation, not just what we *want* to do—or even what other people want us to do. The strength of our moral compass helps us define our character, which determines how people choose to interact with us and contributes to the overall quality of our relationships. A strong moral compass is an essential strength of the leader who desires to consistently do the right things at work and in life.

It is fair to say that consistently using your moral compass can be extremely difficult and challenging. If you have a strong moral compass, does that mean you will never make mistakes or suffer through an ethical or moral stumble? I am afraid not. Instead, those of us with a well-defined set of core values will be able to learn from those failings and use them to make better and more appropriate decisions in the future. In fact, it's often the situations that present adversity and test us that help our moral compass to grow stronger. This has certainly been my experience.

It sometimes feels as if the world has become a challenging

place for men and women of goodwill to thrive. Many of us want to make a positive difference in the world, but we don't know where to begin. *Why not consider the workplace as a place to make a difference?* Displaying courage in the face of our polarized society's obstacles may seem overwhelming, but perhaps we should focus our attention on developing our moral compass and manifesting small acts of bravery to promote ethical and moral principles that are meaningful at work, where we spend so much of our adult lives. These small acts, in turn, can absolutely have a positive ripple effect on the bigger world around us.

Much of what you will read in this book emanates from the moral compass I have endeavored to refine and utilize over the course of my career. I am far from perfect, and I assure you I have stumbled and made mistakes, but I keep on trying—and I encourage you to keep trying too. I promise the positive impact you will make on the people around you will make the effort well worth it.

What steps will you take this week to develop and strengthen your moral compass?

CHAPTER 2

Embracing Simplicity

There is no greatness where there is not simplicity, goodness, and truth.
Leo Tolstoy

Do you ever feel overwhelmed with all the stress, responsibilities, and challenges in your daily life? If I am honest with myself, the times I feel most anxious or stressed are usually caused by my lifelong tendency to overcomplicate things and an inclination toward "busyness." As I grow older, I recognize the wisdom of something my parents often shared with me in my younger days: *Simplify your life.*

Everything about our modern culture involves complexity and unnecessary layers. I long for more opportunities to live in the moment and experience life in "real time" versus the frantic pace I often keep. I want my legacy to be more than "he accomplished more than most"! I don't pretend to have all the answers, but I would like to share my three-step approach to achieve greater simplicity, peace, and a heightened sense of purpose in my life:

- Have clear priorities.
- Practice detachment.
- Serve others.

Step One: Have Clear Priorities

What are your priorities? When I ask this question of other professionals, the answers are typically all over the map. I came into my Christian faith later in life. I went from a compartmentalized approach to living, unsuccessfully attempting to balance work and family, to a life where my faith is first, family is second, and work is third on my list of priorities. Additionally, I work hard at keeping Christ at the center of everything I do, and the result is a more authentic and integrated approach to life where I am the same person at all times.

How Does This Play Out in Your Life?

Faith—Through my active prayer life and worship, I do my best to serve the Lord and make sure He is my top priority. "Lord, help me to simplify my life by learning what you want me to be and becoming that person" (St. Thérèse of Lisieux).

Family—My vocation is to be the best husband and father possible. I serve my family by giving them my time, attention, and love. In our home, family dinner is a priority, as is the commitment my wife and I share in loving our children enough to challenge them with the truth. We have always worked hard to ensure that our children grow up with faith and strong values, and we consider it our duty to serve as role models for them. I also have a responsibility to take care of my health so I can be present in their lives for many years to come.

Work—I focus on sanctifying my work and pursuing excellence. I must remember that my vocation is not my job/career. My job exists to serve my family, not the other way around. My job provides a living for my family and a way to fulfill my mission, but it cannot be allowed to consume me in an unhealthy way.

Having our priorities straight requires intentionality and commitment . . . and a fair amount of courage. We must plan our time, have lines we won't cross, and stick to our principles. Most importantly, those of us who are Christians know we are made for heaven, not this world. We will be judged one day by *how* we lived, not how fast we lived. "If I find in myself a desire which no experience in this world can satisfy, the most probable explanation is that I was made for another world" (C.S. Lewis).

Step Two: Practice Detachment

How do we detach? Does this mean we need to become hermits in a mountainside cabin? Of course not. But we need to acknowledge that we live in a materialistic and consumer-driven world that encourages us to acquire as much stuff as possible, often at the expense of what is truly important. If we can practice real freedom from the blind pursuit of an illusory better life attached to acquiring more material goods we don't need, we will be better prepared to make healthier and more meaningful choices in life. Also, remember that *attaching* ourselves to the right people and activities will further help us *detach* from the negative influences of this world.

Ideas for Pursuing Detachment:

- Let it go. Ask yourself if you really need "it," whatever "it" is. Will the bigger house, bigger car, and other toys truly make you happier? Or are you trying to fill an empty void in yourself with the wrong things?
- Be careful to not let your possessions/hobbies/interests become obstacles between you and your family or you and God.
- Be cognizant of what "enough" really means.
- Resist the siren call of the culture to become someone you are not.
- Recognize the virtue of hard work and reject the easy and responsibility-free life often promised by the world.
- Avoid the "pack mentality" and do what you know is right and true, not what everyone else is doing.
- Value true friends—the ones who challenge you, make you better, and don't require you to compromise who you really are. Be willing to accept having fewer friends in order to enhance your overall relationship health.
- Turn off the noise. Spend less time on your smartphone, TV, internet, podcasts, and talk radio and more time in quiet reflection, prayer, quality time with loved ones, physical exercise, and reading books.
- Frequently express gratitude for your blessings and all you have, and never take your good fortune for granted.

I am challenged on a daily basis by the concept of detachment. It is very difficult to practice, yet when I do make progress in this area, I feel a profound sense of freedom and peace that encourages me to work harder at it every day. The world is constantly trying to pull me in the wrong direction. When I practice detachment from our culture and its more negative influences, I more clearly recognize and value the blessings I have received.

Step Three: Serve Others

What makes you tick? What are you called to do? Knowing *who* you are and *what* you are called to do is a critical component of simplifying your life. When I was in my twenties and thirties, I was focused on climbing the corporate ladder as fast as possible with little understanding of what I would do when I reached the top. As I shared in my third book, *Something More: The Professional's Pursuit of a Meaningful Life*, I walked away from a senior executive role with a billion-dollar restaurant company in my early thirties to run a boutique national executive search firm. In 2013 I launched Serviam Partners (www.ServiamPartners.com), which offers executive coaching and leadership consulting services to companies and senior leaders. These career moves were intentional and part of my ever-increasing desire to simplify my life and fully tap into my skills and passions in the service of others.

Probably the greatest revelation for me over the years has been the sense of peace and joy I feel that only comes from helping and serving other people. Even though I always seek to know, understand, and do God's will in my life, the times I most frequently feel close to achieving this are the times I do something in the service of others.

How Do I Serve Other People?

- As busy as I may be, I strive to make quality time for others.
- Treating others as I wish to be treated is a priority.

- I try to be a good listener.
- I pray for others.
- I engage in civil discussions with those who disagree with me.
- Being candid is a gift when delivered with professionalism and love. I always try and give this gift to those I encounter.
- I connect others to helpful people and resources in my network.
- I try to give not only of my time, but also my talent and treasure to serve and help those less fortunate than I am.
- I always try to add value to my relationships.
- I serve great causes and practice active stewardship with the help of my family and friends.

My giving to others is ultimately a gift right back to me. When I devote myself to helping a person in need, I feel a tremendous sense of fulfillment. My hectic schedule can sometimes get in the way, and I struggle to do all that I desire for others, *but I keep trying.*

Intentionality and Clarity Lead to Simplicity

Do you ever look back on your career? Retrace your steps and reflect on lessons learned? At the beginning of my career, I was a follower, then I became a manager, and then a leader. Now I'm embracing the "influencer" stage of my career. Through my books, talks, coaching, and consulting, I strive to influence positive outcomes for the people I encounter in my life. I make mistakes, but I am clear about my goals and my desire to follow a simpler path, serve others, and live a faith-filled life. The path to get here had many twists and turns, but I was very intentional along the way.

I hope you will reflect on the direction of your life and recognize that the time for embracing a simpler approach to life is *now*—not when you reach retirement. I have observed with gratitude the example my parents set for me of how to live simply, act with humility, and serve others with love and charity. My encouragement to you is, simply put, to *embrace simplicity*. You, your work, and everyone around you will benefit from this life-changing decision. This is often a difficult struggle and countercultural but *get rid of the excess and retain the necessary*. Focus on what is important and have the right priorities. Serve others. *Simplify.*

What is one significant thing you can do to simplify your life in the days ahead?

CHAPTER 3

Let's Be Real

To be yourself in a world that is constantly trying to make you something else is the greatest accomplishment.

RALPH WALDO EMERSON

I have discussed the topic of authenticity with other business professionals for decades. Over the last few years, these conversations have migrated from the importance of allowing others to see the "real" us to guarded discussions about the increasing anxiety people have in today's world regarding being open about and advocating for their beliefs and convictions. In a few very recent discussions with other business leaders, I received blank stares and obvious discomfort when I advocated for being the same person no matter where we were and transparent about our lives with others. *Why is authenticity so uncomfortable?*

I suspect the root cause of this occurred for many of us at a young age. The first time we felt pressure to "fit in" with a particular group in school, we began down the path of conformity that only accelerated as we grew older. In college, we may have heard from professors (or parents) that we need to keep our work, faith, beliefs, and personal lives separate. We may have feared being judged or criticized in those early jobs for sharing anything personal, which only hardens into a compartmentalized mindset as we grow in our careers.

Logic should tell us it is inevitably harmful to suppress our true selves for a sustained period of time, yet people may sometimes feel there is no other option. Do you love being a parent, but feel awkward about discussing your kids and home life at work? Do you care passionately about a particular cause, but refrain from mentioning it for fear of condemnation? Have you struggled with a personal challenge and felt the need to hide it from colleagues lest they judge you? Have you been faced with a difficult situation that conflicts with your principles and values, but remained silent rather than risking criticism? I suspect most of us, myself included, have faced these kinds of situations. I choose to believe that deep down most of us desire to be more consistently authentic, but we may not know how to get there.

Obstacles to Authenticity

Let's address some of the obstacles that may prevent you from being authentic. I am making a basic assumption that you agree on some level that authenticity is important and have a desire to be more open, transparent, and genuine. In my experience, here are some of the obstacles that can inhibit authenticity:

- **Lack of self-awareness.** Do you even know there's a problem?
- **Fear** of people not liking who you truly are. Fear of not fitting in. Fear of being judged. Fear of persecution for

your principles and beliefs. Fear of being passed over for a promotion because you don't fit the corporate mold. Fear of being "canceled" in today's culture.

- **Lack of courage** in defending your opinions and convictions.
- **Attachment** to an income level and lifestyle that requires unhealthy compromise.
- **Conforming** to society's march toward political correctness, restrictions on free speech, and acceptance of things that are in direct conflict with your values and principles.
- **Relaxing** your moral standards because it easier to go along with the crowd than take a stand.
- **Incorrectly believing** that presenting your generic or "fake" self in the workplace is the only path to success.
- **Lack of role models, mentors, and candid friends** who can show you the right approach and help you improve in this area.

This list may be as painful for you to acknowledge as it was for me to write—or you may have a different list. The points raised may be unsettling but confronting them is necessary if we are to pursue and embrace a more authentic life.

How Do We Overcome These Obstacles?

One way forward is to open the aperture about *how* we view the practice of authenticity. It is not enough to simply be authentic; we also have a responsibility to help authenticity thrive in others. Here are **nine positive ways** we can *demonstrate* and *promote* authenticity in daily life:

1. **Treat others with kindness, gratitude, mercy, compassion, fairness, and love.** These can all be powerful manifestations of authenticity if they emanate from our core beliefs and reflect how we truly feel about others.
2. **Be respectful and civil.** I interact with professionals every day who may fundamentally disagree with me on a number of topics, but I always try to respect their points of view, and I ask for that same respect in return. We share our perspectives, experiences, and beliefs in a civil discussion rooted in mutual respect.
3. **Replace angry political arguments with civil discussions about *ideas*.** Let's promote the lost concept of healthy debates. We need more calm dialogue and less screaming in today's polarized world.
4. **Practice active listening.** Good listening skills are essential for promoting authenticity. This is especially true if we make the choice to listen to conflicting opinions with calmness. We should consider responding with thoughtful questions before offering our own opinions in return. If we are truly listening with a desire to learn, we must keep an open mind and even be willing to change our opinion if warranted.
5. **Recognize that diversity of opinion is a good thing.** Conflicting views, beliefs, and opinions contribute to diversity of thought. Without it we risk a frightening monolithic worldview where everyone thinks the same way.
6. **Transparency invites transparency.** Get personal. If we desire someone to open up to us, we should be open about our lives first. In effect, by sharing first we

give the other person "permission" to be open about nonwork-related topics.

7. **Be curious.** Be insatiably curious about others. Learn and remember personal things about them, such as their spouse's and kid's names, hobbies, interests, and birthdays. Open-ended questions like "Where did you grow up?", "What did you do this weekend?", or "What are you doing for vacation this summer?" can be great ways to begin. Authenticity is greatly enhanced by mutual sharing, and sharing thrives in an atmosphere of curiosity.

8. **Build a foundation of trust.** Business relationships will become stronger and more meaningful when you allow others to know, like, and trust you.

9. **Read the room.** Being consistently authentic does not mean always sharing our sad stories or deeply emotional experiences. It does not mean we should share every aspect of our personal lives or topics inappropriate for a particular audience or situation. Use good judgment. Read the room. Be smart.

We must challenge the fear that somehow being real is a bad thing. It may be uncomfortable and create some opposition in the short term from individuals not used to it. However, practicing transparency, engaging in honest and open dialogue, and always placing our principles and ethics before advancing our careers will bring us greater success in every aspect of our lives. I have seen the positive fruits of this in my own life and the lives of countless other business leaders. *I would also argue that the most authentic business leaders I know are also the most inspiring and by far the most successful.*

I am sharing this from my perspective as a father, husband, person of faith, and business owner who is very involved in the community. You may have different perspectives and views on this topic, but I believe anyone can find relevant value in what I am sharing. Maybe we should stop thinking that being ourselves, holding differing views on important subjects, or resisting the expectations of the surrounding culture are somehow bad things. In the business world, we should all seek the freedom to no longer sacrifice our uniqueness and who we truly are on the altar of political expediency.

After you read this chapter, take some time to consider whether you are being authentic to those around you. Commit to setting a good example for others, especially the generations coming after you, by being unafraid to be your true self. Remember that a lifetime of little compromises at work (and elsewhere) eventually adds up to an overwhelming denial of who we really are. Authenticity is not easy, but it's necessary if we want to change the growing challenges around the simple practice of being our real selves. Our acts of authenticity in the workplace, exercised with *prudence* and *good judgment*, can dramatically improve the quality of business conversations, foster trusting relationships, unleash hidden potential, and potentially improve business results.

With confidence and a sense of purpose, let's all try to be a little more authentic to the people around us.

How will you show up as more authentic to
the people in your life, beginning tomorrow?

CHAPTER 4

Credibility Matters

Never forget that credibility can be earned or lost every day of your life, and you need to take it seriously.

MY FATHER'S ADVICE TO ME AS A YOUNG PROFESSIONAL

Credibility is important. It is one of the most important things a professional must possess to grow in their career and be successful. True credibility can't be bought, and nobody should feel they are entitled to it. It must be earned, and it requires self-awareness, hard work, time, and patience. Once earned, credibility cannot be taken for granted; it can be lost, damaged, or enhanced by our actions every single day. Credibility should matter to everyone, regardless of their age or station in life, but this chapter is primarily written for college students and new business professionals interested in growing their careers and making a positive mark in the business world.

One of the first things to understand about credibility is that your perception of your own credibility is likely *not* always the same as the perception of those around you. Like it or not, you are being scrutinized with "silent judgment" by those who have a significant say in you getting your internship, first job, next job, or promotion at work. This is the hard truth: from the very first encounter, you are being evaluated on a host of areas that may have nothing to do with your résumé, educational background, or current work experience. During interviews or networking conversations, decision-makers in the business world are gauging your likability, integrity, values, professionalism, ability to do a great job, how you will mesh with the team, how you will fit into the company culture, etc. Their willingness to help you, advocate for you, hire you, or promote you is based on the credibility you show through characteristics you exhibit in your personal and professional life. If you have perceived credibility, this reduces their risk and builds trust in your abilities.

How Do We Show Up as Credible?

I am fortunate in my professional and personal life to engage with college students and new professionals on a frequent basis. As I work with these aspiring leaders, I often share these **ten helpful and proven tips** for making a good first impression and showing up as credible:

1. **Be courteous, respectful, punctual, and grateful.** These are table stakes and fundamental. A huge part of being considered credible during a first professional encounter is showing basic courtesy, respect, punctuality, and gratitude. Always being on time, saying please, thank you, sir, ma'am, and sending handwritten thank-you notes after meetings are concepts that never go out of style and always enhance credibility.

2. **Be responsive.** When communicating with anyone, especially in the business world, being responsive in a timely manner is very important. I strongly encourage use of the twenty-four-hour rule in all communication responses. Waiting any longer to respond signals a lack of interest and creates a bad impression with professionals on the other end. Also, make sure all communications, especially via email, are professionally written and free of grammatical errors.

3. **Follow through.** Always, always, always do what you say you will do—and *never* make excuses. Honor your commitments. If you say you will get back to someone tomorrow, then do it. If you say you will take care of a task or assume ownership of something, then do it. Lack of follow through and excuse-making is a red alert signal that perhaps you cannot be trusted, and this negatively impacts your credibility.

4. **Be sincere and vulnerable.** True credibility comes from a place of sincerity and can't be faked. Be real and don't be afraid to show vulnerability. For example, admitting that you don't know the answer to a question or sharing that you are sometimes uncomfortable with networking can help you gain credibility with more senior leaders.

5. **Always do the right thing.** Always live with integrity. Live by your values, principles, and code of ethics in all areas of your life. Be honest and accountable for your actions in all situations. This is hopefully core to who you are, and you should never be afraid of sacrificing a little professional success for the knowledge that you consistently do the right thing.

The most credible leaders I know lead with their values front and center.

6. **Cultivate a professional image.** In the age of virtual meetings, many of us have gotten a little relaxed in our dress code/image. When you are a student or new professional looking to establish yourself as credible, *go the other direction.* Always dress professionally and be well-groomed. This doesn't mean you have to wear a tie or a nice dress to every encounter, but avoid jeans, t-shirts, or anything else that indicates you are less than professional. Also, make sure your résumé looks professional. Avoid sounding inappropriately familiar at the beginning of a new professional relationship, and never use slang or inappropriate language. First impressions really do matter.

7. **Be careful with your online presence.** In today's polarized and politically charged world, be cautious about what you post online. Companies often research your online footprint, and an inappropriate meme or an angry comment can negatively impact your credibility, career growth, and even employability in a way that is easily avoidable.

8. **Tell your story well.** Every personal work experience, volunteer activity, participation on a sports team, travel experience, and college course is part of your compelling personal story, regardless of your age. This is also true of where you grew up, adversity you may have faced, and successes you have achieved. How well you weave these pieces of your story together and share them with others is a key part of being seen as credible and relatable to others.

9. **Do consistently good work.** It should go without saying that your work should speak for itself. Let your consistent hard work and excellent results do your talking for you. This is a foundational part of professional credibility, and all new professionals have the same opportunity to shine.

10. **Volunteer, but do not overcommit.** Ask for the difficult tasks and the jobs nobody else wants. Endure longer hours to finish the tough projects. Volunteering can and should also mean spending time in the community supporting great causes. All of this enhances credibility, but be careful to not overcommit yourself. Use good judgment and don't overextend yourself to the point that your day job suffers.

How Do We Seek Help with Credibility from Others?

Personal credibility is a worthy goal for all of us, but it is not a journey we have to travel alone. I have greatly benefited from the help and wise counsel of more senior leaders, friends, and family in my career who have played helpful roles as I strove to be more credible over the years. Here are **three important ways** to enlist the help of others:

1. **Ask for candid feedback.** Are you credible? Consistently go to people in your life who will be brutally honest with you. Give them permission to tell you what they really think and ask them if you come across as credible. Get their specific guidance on what you can do to improve. This courageous practice can help you grow and stay on track.

2. **Seek out mentors and advocates.** I benefited a great deal from helpful mentors early in my career who taught me through their personal examples how to authentically grow in credibility, and I will always be grateful to these amazing men and women. I also encountered advocates along the way who went to bat for me regarding new jobs, promotions, and other career opportunities. I had to earn their trust and advocacy through diligence, hard work, and results, but these key leaders made connections for me and helped open doors that I might not have been able to open on my own. *Helpful Tip:* When someone does something like this for you, they are taking a chance and putting their own credibility at risk. Go to great lengths to honor their kind act and *never* do anything to make them regret it.

3. **Build a strong network of relationships.** Your goal over time is to build a deep and diverse network of trusted professionals and colleagues who will provide you with ongoing mentoring, advice, and candid feedback as you progress at your job and in your career. *Always seek to associate with other professionals who are credible.* The key is to work hard at getting to know as many people as you can on a more personal level. These contacts and connections can be critical mentors, sounding boards for your ideas, and potential advocates for you and your work throughout the organization. Demonstrate to them your motivation, commitment, and relevant expertise, and whenever possible, find ways you can be of service to them and help them with their work.

I wrote this chapter out of a sincere desire to help and support college students and new professionals who may not be hearing enough of this advice in school or the workplace. What I have shared comes from three decades of experience, and I promise that these ideas and approaches work. I hope it is obvious to more senior leaders who are reading this chapter that you and I have to be mindful of *our* credibility as well. We can never take it for granted, and much of the advice here applies to us as well. I also hope we will actively engage with this next generation of leaders and advise them on the importance of credibility—and most importantly, *give them great role models to follow.*

Is there someone in your circle of influence who is just beginning their career? How might you model professional credibility for them? If you believe changes are needed after reading this chapter, how might you improve your own credibility?

CHAPTER 5

The Joy of Work

Lessons from a Young Man with Autism

There can be no joy in living without joy in work.
ST. THOMAS AQUINAS

My oldest son Alex has high-functioning autism. He is a wonderful and bright young man with many gifts, balanced to some degree by social quirkiness and other challenges resulting from his autism. When he graduated from high school, my wife and I decided he was not yet ready for the rigors of college and instead focused on helping him find employment and increasing his independence.

He has been employed since he graduated from high school by a global retailer in one of their stores near our home. He works part-time and absolutely loves his job. The store employees have embraced him as one of their own, and he has thrived in this supportive environment, surrounded by good people who genuinely like and care about him. The store assigned Alex a longtime employee as his coach when he first began working there, and along with other senior team members, this wonderful gentleman ensures that Alex stays on track and receives the proper training he needs to be successful.

Alex has found purpose and self-confidence in his work. At home he regales our family with stories about his day and interactions with customers, some of whom he knows from our church and the surrounding community. Alex takes his job seriously and is always on time. He works hard and follows the rules. He never complains about the work. He offers to help other team members even if it is not his responsibility to do so. He takes pride in being an employee of this company, and he shares this pride with others he encounters outside of work.

What can we learn from a young man with autism who truly loves his job? I often reflect on this topic and can offer **five impactful lessons** that have made a difference to me and others who know my son:

1. **Focus on the task in front of you; live in the moment.** Alex isn't thinking about promotions or his next job. He is trying to do the best job he can with the tasks he has been given. He is fully present and focused at work. How often do we lose sight of this and get wrapped up in longing for something we don't have versus simply doing our best work?

2. **Work colleagues can be an extension of your family.** Alex has embraced his co-workers as his extended family. They are his friends, and he knows them all by name. They, in turn, have welcomed and cared for him as a member of their work family. Do you ever consider your work colleagues in this light? What

if you more readily welcomed new employees or those who don't look, think, or act like you?

3. **Griping is not productive.** Alex has been employed for over four years, and I have never heard him complain about his job—*not even once*. There is a place for constructive criticism or comments if the desire is to make things better, but how often does this turn into unproductive griping at the water cooler with a work colleague?

4. **What about your company makes you proud?** Alex knows he is liked and accepted at his company. He feels like he is contributing and making a difference. He is constantly learning new things. He makes enough money to do the things he enjoys in his free time. In a simplistic way, Alex feels proud to be part of his organization and tells everyone where he works. What makes you proud about your employer? Can you see past the negatives (and we all have them) to see the good? Do you proudly share this good with others?

5. **No job or task is too small.** Alex is a "worker bee" and does some of the more mundane tasks in his workplace. But he sees his role as important. He is contributing in his small way to the success of the operation, and it makes him feel necessary and needed. Don't lose sight of the importance of the little things, the routine tasks, and the unglamorous jobs. They all count, and it truly matters that these jobs are done well.

Alex is a young adult with autism, but if I am honest, he is more advanced than I am when it comes to how he views work. He works for the joy of it and the feeling of purpose it gives him. He knows his job, and he does the best he can despite his challenges. He has found a way to contribute to society when many would have assumed it was impossible because of his disability.

I have shared with friends that I should never allow myself to have a bad day compared to what Alex faces. I see him embrace with enthusiasm a world that is often alien, difficult, and even hostile because of his autism. Despite these challenges, he does his best with a smile on his face. He gets up and goes to work. He finds joy in it.

Alex inspires me to be more joyful, and I am very proud of him.

How do you derive joy from your work? Who are your joyful role models? Are you a role model for others?

CHAPTER 6

Live Life Gratefully

When it comes to life, the critical thing is whether you take things for granted or take them with gratitude.

G.K. CHESTERTON

At a very young age, my parents constantly urged me to always say thank you in response to any kindness or friendly words shared in my direction. For many years, I saw this advice from my parents as simply good manners and what people were supposed to do. In my mid-teen years, I was mature enough to observe the heartfelt sincerity my parents always showed when they said thank you to others, offered prayers of thanks, or expressed appreciation for the simple blessings in their lives— and how different this was from my perfunctory use of the words. They really meant it, and I began to understand that their use of the words *thank you* transcended mere courtesy and clearly meant something much more meaningful and powerful to them. What I observed my parents practicing so well was the beginning of my deeper understanding of the concept of *gratitude*.

My parents were wonderful role models and teachers in many ways and helping me learn to be grateful was an amazing gift that I work at demonstrating every day. My wife and I try very hard to model a life of gratefulness for our sons and for those we encounter each day, and this ongoing effort has absolutely transformed us.

What Are Some of the Fruits of Gratitude?

- We desire less when we are truly grateful for what we already have in our lives.
- People who are grateful for what they have are more generous to those in need.
- Gratitude requires a positive frame of mind, which contributes to greater overall happiness. There cannot be happiness without gratitude.
- Consistently practicing gratitude with others results in a ripple effect; those experiencing our gratitude pay it forward to the people they encounter.
- We positively impact and grow our relationships with a grateful attitude.
- Gratitude is a healthy substitute for resentment, envy, jealousy, and greed (see point number one).

Many people, often myself included, find it challenging to consistently act with gratitude. The great writer G. K. Chesterton observed: "Gratitude, being nearly the greatest of human duties, is also nearly the most difficult." What are best practices we can follow to help us be more grateful?

Gratitude Best Practices

- **Learn to be grateful for your challenges, not just your blessings**. Look at adversity as a source of helpful lessons rather than frustrating burdens to carry.

- **Express gratitude at every opportunity.** "I am grateful . . ." "I appreciate . . ." and a simple "Thank you" can never be overused and should be shared throughout the day when appropriate opportunities arise.

- **Make it memorable.** Send a handwritten note of gratitude whenever possible.

- **Be intentional.** Place a reminder on the calendar each Friday morning to express gratitude for the people and blessings you have experienced during the week.

- **Be grateful for EVERYTHING.** "Cultivate the habit of being grateful for every good thing that comes to you, and to give thanks continuously. And because all things have contributed to your advancement, you should include all things in your gratitude" (Ralph Waldo Emerson).

- **Always give thanks to God.** Be grateful to God for the gift of your life, for air in your lungs, the shining sun on your face, and for all Creation. Share this gratitude in prayer throughout the day. "God's generous presence in our lives lays claim to a form of gratitude that is never satisfied by the mere recitation of thanks but requires us to express our gratitude in action. The kind of gratitude that God is hoping to find is one that includes a bond of friendship and a commitment to service" (Donald DeMarco, *The Many Faces of Virtue*).

As you consider how to go about living your life and interacting with those you encounter each day, why not choose the gratitude approach? Make the commitment and watch your life absolutely change for the better.

Live gratefully and you will *never* regret it.

At the end of each day this week, write down three things you are grateful for and at least two ways you have practiced gratitude.

PART TWO

Showing Up Well
at Work

CHAPTER 7

A Road Map to Candid Work Conversations

Great teams do not hold back with one another. They are unafraid to air their dirty laundry. They admit their mistakes, their weaknesses, and their concerns without fear of reprisal.

Patrick Lencioni, Author of
The Five Dysfunctions of a Team

You're in a staff meeting listening to a work colleague drone on about his success on a recent project, but you know he is actually behind and over budget. *What do you do?*

One of your direct reports has a few self-limiting behaviors that are impeding her career growth and negatively affecting the team, but you don't want to hurt her feelings. Performance reviews are coming up, and you need to rate her work. *How will you handle the situation?*

A colleague lacks self-awareness about the negative reputation he has earned in the company. He doesn't work for you, but you want to help him get back on track. *How will you approach him?*

One of your company's senior executives consistently asks

for feedback, but you doubt his sincerity. A business problem arises that you know will reflect poorly on decisions made by this leader. *Will you have the courage to speak up?*

I observe and hear about scenarios like these playing out in companies almost every day. Direct, honest feedback about performance and other important topics has become a lost art in many corporate environments, and this has given way to coddling, surface conversations, and conflict workarounds. A pervasive lack of candid conversations in business has a significant negative psychological, cultural, and financial impact on leaders, teams, and entire organizations when left unaddressed. Lack of candor causes distrust, stifles innovation, slows decision-making, and hampers productivity. The desire to avoid conflict is understandable, but it's one of the most debilitating factors in business today, and this behavior exacts a steep price. If the problem is as widespread as I believe it to be, what do we do about it?

Why Is Candor Difficult?

Let's make an effort to understand *why* we have a candor problem in the workplace today. I have identified **five key causes**:

1. **Lack of self-awareness.** Are you and I aware that we might have a problem in this area? Has anyone told us? Are we sincerely seeking critical and honest feedback about how we come across to others?

2. **PC work environments.** A too-polite veneer often signals an overly politicized workplace. Colleagues who are afraid to speak honestly to people's faces often do

it behind their backs. A fear of saying the wrong thing or being misunderstood by those around us has placed a significant restriction on meaningful dialogue in today's workplace and instead often encourages surface conversations at the expense of candid ones.

3. **Fear of hurting the feelings of others.** Candor is typically and incorrectly assumed to be negative or hurtful instead of the helpful gift it truly is when delivered well. We may struggle to navigate the tension between delivering an honest and helpful message versus hurting the feelings of our colleagues.

4. **Fear of repercussions.** If I am candid and say the wrong thing to the wrong person, what will happen to me? Will my career growth or even my job be at risk if I speak up?

5. **Not sure what to say.** Surprisingly, this is one of the most common obstacles to speaking with more candor at work. I find that many well-intentioned professionals desire to speak more candidly with their colleagues, but they wish to do it in a way that will be accepted with minimal frustration and pain. They simply lack the words and overthink what should necessarily be a respectful, clear, and helpful conversation.

When I shared with a friend my intention to write on this topic, he assumed it would be some sort of "Candor Manifesto" meant to move every company's culture in the direction of increased candor. I am skeptical of company-wide initiatives of this magnitude and instead place my faith in the sincere efforts of individuals who are willing to embrace healthy and meaningful change. You see, I believe the best way to positively impact our work cultures and make candor more attractive is through the intentional actions of each reader of this book. If each of us will subscribe to the "pebble in a pond" concept, our individual embrace and application of candor will ripple throughout our organizations. We must model the behavior we wish to see in everybody else. How do we do this?

Embrace New Concepts and Approaches

First, I would encourage each of us to consider these basic concepts:

- Candid conversations do *not* have to be ugly or painful.
- All candid feedback, if given respectfully, is a gift. "Candor is a compliment; it implies equality. It's how true friends talk" (Peggy Noonan, author and *Wall Street Journal* columnist).
- If we assume good intent and think of the person giving us honest feedback as helpful and generous rather than critical, we become less defensive and more open to changing our behavior.
- In order to initiate effective candid conversations, let's try to orient our thinking this way: "I desire to be helpful, and I care enough about you to tell you the truth."
- Candid conversations are best served with clear, simple, direct language that includes relevant examples. The calling card of dishonest talk is flowery or ambiguous language.

There are numerous misperceptions about candor, and we often have an unhealthy fear of what it is and is not. In fact, I would argue that candor is a helpful weapon against fear and *not* something in itself to be feared. *Candor* comes from the Latin word *candere*, which means "to shine or illuminate." Perhaps to be candid means we must be courageous enough to shine a light into dark places. Embracing the concepts above is part of the solution, but we need to also be intentional about changing our behaviors.

Twelve Best Practices for Facilitating Candid Work Conversations

1. **Model it.** Be willing to model the behavior you wish to see in others. Are you setting a good and consistent example for those around you? Do you both speak with candor and receive it well from others?

2. **Admit mistakes.** One of the best ways to begin a candid conversation is to be humble enough to admit you've made a mistake and own the consequences. How often do we see leaders do this today?

3. **Never punish; always reward.** Don't shoot the messenger! If someone has the courage to speak up about uncomfortable topics, publicly acknowledge and thank them for their honesty. Encourage others to follow their example.

4. **Be courteous and ask permission.** Whenever I need to deliver what may be taken as difficult feedback, I ask permission first. I simply say, "May I have permission to be candid?" In all the years I have asked this question, nobody has ever said no. The other person enters into

a psychological "contract" with me, knowing I am going to share something they may not like, but they appreciate my courtesy and are prepared to receive what I wish to share.

5. **Give permission.** Let everyone around you know you are sincerely open to hearing their candid thoughts. Rather than putting someone on the spot and asking for feedback (which often inspires anxiety), try giving those around you blanket permission to come to you in private when they have something to share. When receiving candid feedback, always thank the person who offered it and avoid being defensive.

6. **Be respectful.** An offshoot of my fourth point about asking for permission is to always be respectful of your audience if you wish your message to be more readily accepted. Egos can be easily bruised in these exchanges and being respectful is a great best practice you can utilize to defuse the tension your directness may cause. You should both deliver and receive messages this way. Use phrases like "Are you open to a different perspective?", "I might suggest . . . ," or "Please consider this . . ." when offering feedback. Where applicable, express sincere praise for things done well in addition to giving feedback on challenges or ways to improve.

7. **Be constructive and helpful.** Negative feedback can sometimes hurt, but learn to view it is a gift aimed at helping the recipient improve performance and avoid future mistakes. One way to be more helpful is to be clear about the challenging behaviors you have observed and the suggestions you offer for improvement. Stay

away from ambiguous language and use concrete examples whenever possible.

8. **Avoid embarrassment.** It will sometimes be necessary in meetings to have difficult conversations with your colleagues, so be mindful that you do not want to embarrass them while still delivering an honest and helpful message. There is a huge difference between picking projects apart and picking *people* apart.

9. **Be more curious.** We often miss opportunities for candid and substantive conversations because we fail to ask questions and show genuine curiosity. Asking probing questions of others rather than merely stating our opinions can provide an opportunity to bring difficult topics to light. Examples can look like this: "Jack, do you feel like you are executing on the project the way you hoped?" or "Rachel, I am concerned that we will miss our revenue targets this month. What do you see as the obstacles in your team's way and how can I help you overcome them?"

10. **Candor is best when delivered in person.** As a rule, nothing that is emotional, awkward, or subject to misinterpretation should ever be conveyed via email. If it all possible, I would encourage delivering candid feedback in private to ensure maximum receptivity. Candor is best suited to in-person conversations or by phone if necessary.

11. **Promote candor through team accountability.** Real collaboration is unlikely to occur when people don't trust one another to speak with candor. Suggest to your team that candor be required in every team or staff

meeting and be sure to model it for others. Take turns holding one another accountable for this behavior and do not be afraid to respectfully call out your colleagues when someone avoids addressing difficult issues.

12. **No jerks allowed.** There is no place for bullying or boorish behavior in this vision of a candid workplace. Demeaning our colleagues in any way should not be tolerated in cultures that claim to value their employees.

In my own experience, I have found that my effectiveness in having candid conversations with anyone is predicated on the other person trusting that I am sincerely trying to be helpful. I own the responsibility to earn that trust, and I do so through investing heavily in building authentic relationships with my business network. There are no tricks, gimmicks, or hidden agendas, but there is a lot of hard work (as illustrated by the twelve best practices above) to ensure that I am doing my part in encouraging mutually respectful candid conversations. These conversations provide a great opportunity to apply the Golden Rule and treat others as I wish to be treated.

The Fruits of Candor and a Call to Action

If you sincerely implement these best practices with consistency, people in all areas of your life will begin to seek you out for insights and advice because they can count on you to deliver what so few people in their circles are willing to provide. Whether you are a subordinate or a manager, the key is to take some sort of action to increase the candor and flow of honest dialogue in your organization. If you do nothing, you are just reinforcing unproductive patterns. But if you are willing to do *something*, you can help trigger a cycle of increasing self-awareness, personal growth, and elevated performance for yourself and others—and create a much more enjoyable and trusting work environment for everyone.

Professionals who intentionally embrace candor will encourage, and even reward, straight talk from their colleagues and teams. They understand that whatever momentary discomfort they may experience is more than offset by the fact that better information and honest conversations help them make better decisions. Unfortunately, there is no easy way to institutionalize candor on a large scale. Candid behavior at the top of the leadership chain is critical, but lasting change in this area requires sustained effort, focus, and constant vigilance from each of us, regardless of our title. It also requires a sincere willingness to own our behavior and make the necessary changes. This is the clear challenge I am asking each of us to accept as a positive step toward making an impactful difference in our workplaces today.

> *Will you take on the "candor challenge"?*
> *Commit to these two helpful steps:*

- Identify and reflect on at least two reasons why candor may be difficult for you.
- Practice at least three of these candor best practices this week.

CHAPTER 8

Clarity Matters

Clarity is the preoccupation of the effective leader.
If you do nothing else as a leader, be clear.
Marcus Buckingham, AUTHOR

As I began writing this chapter, I reflected on the conversations I have been having with clients and other business leaders over the past few years. I was struck by a central theme that seems to be popping up in most of them: the importance of *clarity* and the negative impact the lack of clarity has on teams and organizations. The primary reason this issue is hitting my radar is a key question I ask my clients every January: *What are the biggest challenges for you and your team that you wish to address more effectively this year?* Consistently, I hear a desire to improve accountability, increase efficiency, foster greater ownership, improve communication, and achieve better overall results. I would suggest the answer to all of these challenges—or at least the beginning of the answer—can be found by dramatically improving *clarity*.

Why is clarity so difficult to consistently achieve? One big reason is that we may be too busy racing from task to task rather than thoughtfully creating clarity in our spheres of influence at work and requiring clarity from others. *Why are we so busy?* Perhaps it is because we are negatively affected by the inefficiency created by the lack of clarity and the dysfunctional way it takes over our calendars with repetitive meetings and calls to rehash the same conversations over and over (visualize a hamster on a wheel). Perhaps we have accepted the lack of clarity as "the way we do things around here." Maybe, just maybe, the challenge with clarity is connected to a lack of *candor.* Are we willing to clearly and publicly identify issues in front of our colleagues and commit to greater accountability with deadlines? Are we willing to respectfully but candidly question how we do things within our teams and organizations in an effort to make them better?

If clarity is an issue for us, our teams, and our companies, how do we address it? Let's begin by focusing on **five types of clarity** that can positively impact decision-making, the way business meetings are conducted, overall efficiency, and execution:

1. **Do you have clarity around the "why"?** Why is this project necessary and what will it solve? Why are you having this meeting? Is there an agenda? Do you know why you are here and what your team needs to get done? The "why" question is the most important one and can be applied to almost every action and decision. If you can clearly answer the "why," can you connect it back to your overall strategy? Consider how to better incorporate the "why" question into your daily routine

and connect it to better outcomes with the people you encounter each day.

2. **Do you have clarity on tasks and deadlines?** What specifically are you asking others to do? What are the details? When exactly is the assignment/task due? For example, sending someone into battle to "hurry up and fix the company sales problem" is setting them up for failure. We need to marry specificity to actions and tasks. Consider this example: "Mike will be creating a process to increase revenue by 5 percent in professional services before the end of Q2, and he will have his action plan on how to do this ready to present in our next staff meeting." Doing this aspect of clarity well is directly connected to dramatically improving accountability.

3. **Do you have clarity of ownership?** I see a rampant problem in companies today with lack of clarity around ownership. A common scenario is that a leader will challenge the team to do something significant in a meeting but fail to assign specific ownership or ask someone to step up and publicly take ownership. Confusion and chaos are the result; more than one person may assume they own solving the problem and time and resources are wasted with duplicative efforts. Clarifying *who* owns it should always be a given.

4. **Do you have role clarity?** This aspect of clarity goes beyond task ownership and is more about defining the sandbox you play in, what you are accountable for, and how you will specifically do your job, contribute to a project, or help solve a problem faced by the team. Role clarity also defines the overall scope and responsibilities

of your job. There will always be some unavoidable degree of overlap in certain roles, but an emphasis on clarifying roles, duties, and decision-making rights (in writing) can make this problem more palatable and reduce unnecessary friction.

5. **Do you have clarity of communication?** Ambiguity and an overall lack of clarity in leadership communication often contribute to misunderstandings, inefficiency, and poor execution. Every email or text from a leader needs to create clarity, not confusion or chaos. Who is my audience? What am I trying to convey? Have I given them clear action steps? Did I explain the "why"? The thoughts below are primarily associated with improving business meetings, but I am focusing on this because most of the communication dysfunction I observe takes place in poorly run meetings and the resulting follow-up. Consider this short list of action steps for every business meeting:

   - Never have a meeting without a clear agenda, ideally shared forty-eight hours in advance.
   - Always assign a scribe to take notes (rotate this assignment on team), specifically listing a summary of key points from the meeting, task ownership, the specific tasks in detail, and due dates.
   - Disseminate meeting notes to all participants within twenty-four hours of meeting.
   - *Helpful Tip:* Chapter 11 goes deeper into addressing dysfunctional business meetings.

I recognize this may seem like a lot of hard work when you are likely very busy. But I encourage you to consider that embracing greater clarity will actually reduce your workload, make you more efficient, and enhance your ability to execute. If you have become the proverbial hamster on the wheel, it is time to get off.

Keep at it, and the clarity you can offer those within your sphere of influence *will* improve.

Try these practical approaches, beginning this week:

- Are *you* good at clarity? Ask for *candid feedback* from colleagues.
- Ask yourself each of the five clarity questions we posed in this session *before* big decisions, certainly before and during every meeting, and before communicating with your colleagues.
- Create space on your calendar to be more thoughtful about clarity.
- Don't worry if your attempts at clarity are not perfect. Focus on simply making the effort and *go for small wins.*
- Frequently discuss the topic with your colleagues in meetings and promote greater accountability to get it right.
- Try to be the role model for everyone else.
- Always remember that every email, call, meeting, and decision has a *ripple effect* and *real consequences.* Please reflect on this and act accordingly . . . *with clarity.*

CHAPTER 9

Living Life in Real Time

Yesterday is gone. Tomorrow has not yet come.
We have only today. Let us begin.
St. Teresa of Calcutta (Mother Teresa)

Up until 2012, I would say that I maximized my days as well as anyone and was always comfortable juggling multiple projects and tasks. My business was thriving, my books were selling well, and I had achieved a small modicum of success by the world's standard. But then I began to recognize that I was often missing out on the truly important things in life. My hectic pace, which mirrored the pace of so many other professionals in my circle, began to negatively impact the *quality* of time I was spending with clients, friends, and loved ones. My crazy schedule and the countless meetings I attended each week began to blur together, and I felt that I was not being truly present to the people who richly deserved my full attention, especially my wonderful wife and two sons. The pace I was keeping also had a deeply negative impact on my ability to gather my thoughts, reflect on lessons learned, and ponder the future. This epiphany, which occurred in the last few days of 2012, became the basis for my commitment to slow down and begin living life in "real time."

I have become very intentional the last several years about pursuing this concept and have shared my journey with clients, business colleagues, friends, and family. In these conversations I am frequently asked to explain the meaning of *living life in real time*. Here is how I have come to define it:

> For busy professionals, living life in real time is about slowing down and savoring the meaningful moments we all encounter each day to be more fully present for our work colleagues, friends, and especially our families. If done well, it means we have embraced a refreshingly radical re-prioritization of how we spend our time; we have learned to consistently say no to the unnecessary and embrace the necessary in order to create more quality time for ourselves and those we encounter. We have also learned to be reflective about our past and thoughtful about the future in the hard-fought moments we create in our busy schedules.

As I continue to refine this idea and discuss it with other professionals, **five central truths** have emerged that are important to acknowledge:

1. More activity and longer to-do lists don't necessarily make us more effective, productive, or happy.
2. A hectic pace and filling up our work calendars are often based on our misperceptions about the expectations of those around us and the senior leaders we desire to impress.

3. There is certainly nothing wrong with hard work! But it must be balanced with paying adequate attention to our emotional, mental, and physical health.

4. We control our calendars—our calendars do not control us. We must admit that our calendars are overscheduled because we have likely allowed it to happen. We must fight back and take control!

5. Many of us are simply uncomfortable with anything less than a full schedule. Calendar holes often trigger feelings of guilt and anxiety. Instead, we should recognize them as gifts of time for reflection, strategic thinking, physical exercise (if possible), or simply time to rest, catch our breath, and refuel.

What Are the Fruits of a Life Lived in Real Time?

- As we slow down our pace and gain better focus, our teams and peers should see a greater time investment from us in helping with their professional and personal growth. How often do we intentionally take the time to invest in others with our current hectic schedules? We become more thoughtful about engaging with our colleagues and actively practice random acts of praise, kindness, and gratitude, or RAPKG, which you can read more about in chapter 13.

- Clearer priorities, less stress at work, less time spent on the trivial, and a commitment to what is important will translate into more time being present with our families, friends, and in serving the community when we are away from the workplace.

- The quality of our work improves as we focus more

time and attention on our highest priorities versus a shotgun approach where multiple areas of our lives receive marginal attention at best.

- We become more reflective *and* effective as we reclaim time to consider our past actions and learn valuable lessons we can apply in the future. Over the course of my career, I've realized that numerous mistakes could have been avoided if I had simply devoted more time to reflect and learn from my past experiences.

- We are more likely to enjoy our jobs and stay in them longer if we can reduce stress and find more meaningful ways to approach the workday.

- There are strong, effective, grounded, and respected business leaders out there who are pretty good at living life in real time. I know several, and I bet you do as well. This should demonstrate to all of us that business success can be compatible with prioritizing the meaningful things in life.

Let's look at how we can make practical progress in attaining this "life in real time." Here are **eight best practices** to consider:

1. **Take control of the calendar.** Be more discerning about which meetings you attend. Learn to say NO when necessary rather than agreeing to every meeting request. Block out meeting-free periods on your calendar and train those around you that you usually will not be available during these windows. Learn to identify and thwart *time thieves* who want to take over your calendar.

2. **Conduct a schedule audit.** Review your calendar over a two-week period from the last year (and make this an intentional practice every quarter). Make note of the meetings you attended where your presence was not really needed or the meetings you led which could have been shortened or avoided altogether. Use this information to help plan where you spend time in the coming year.

3. **Build "air" into your schedule.** Try adding a thirty-minute window to your schedule every day for two weeks. Do not fill it with busy work, but instead take some quiet time with the door closed to collect your thoughts or map out a few ideas on a white board. Maybe you can take a walk outside or have a meaningful conversation with a team member. If you survive this change (and you will), gradually increase the time the following week until you attain one hour a day. *Helpful Tip*: I have taken one whole day away from my office every quarter for several years to conduct a personal mini retreat where all I do is read, write, brainstorm, reflect on the past, and think about the future. This time is critical for me to refuel, create, and be more effective as a leader.

4. **Schedule *everything* that is important.** In my life, if it is not on my calendar, it is not likely to occur. *Everything* goes on my calendar. This includes when I need to be home for dinner, time for writing, time for brainstorming, meetings with my network of clients and friends over coffee or lunch, my prayer life, time for the gym, etc. I even have reminders to call my wife and

children to tell them I love them. Everything important gets scheduled.

5. **Practice *radical prioritization* every week.** Focus on a Top 5 list of the biggest priorities and actively work to accomplish them. If everything is a priority, then nothing is a priority. Don't spread yourself so thin that you are giving a marginal effort to multiple tasks. Focus on being excellent at fewer things. More can sometimes be less!

6. **Set clear boundaries.** When does the workday end and family/personal time begin? If the lines feel blurred for you, here are two ideas to draw clearer boundaries around your schedule: 1) Don't send or respond to nonemergency emails after 6:00 p.m. Monday through Friday or on the weekends. *These can wait.* Every sent email creates an expectation to the recipient that you are "on" and working, which perpetuates the problem of after-hours email. 2) If someone wishes to schedule a nonemergency call or meeting with you after the time you have set as a "boundary," *politely say no and offer them alternatives* that work better for your schedule.

7. **Go device-free from time to time.** Put the smartphone in another room or turn it off during family time. One of my clients gives his iPhone to his wife from 6:00 to 9:00 p.m. each weekday evening to help him focus on family dinner and quality time with his loved ones. Do whatever it takes! If we are to truly be present for others, reflect more, think more, and enjoy our relationships more, we need to learn to put away the

devices. ***Helpful Tip:*** Consider carrying a journal with you at all times and write down your thoughts when you have free moments (instead of looking at your phone). This has been a personal practice of mine for more than twenty years.

8. **Recognize that time is a finite resource.** Time is a finite resource, yet we often foolishly behave as if there is an endless supply of it to accomplish everything on our daily to-do lists. We need to embrace the idea of creating space in our days or run the risk of being less effective, less efficient, and experiencing burnout. This is one of the most effective forms of self-care, but also one of the most overlooked.

Of all the resolutions I have taken on during my life, the effort to live life in real time has given me the most satisfaction. I am grateful for the appreciation of friends when I have slowed down enough to listen and be truly present for them. My family has been the recipient of the quality time I have freed up by saying no to unnecessary business travel and honoring a long-standing commitment to be present for them on evenings and weekends. They also know dinnertime is sacred in our house.

My business has thrived by focusing on quality versus quantity. I am grateful to live my life by a different set of rules that is somewhat countercultural. This allows me to have more balance, reduced stress, time to reflect, time to dream, and quality time for the people in my life. I know for certain that I do not want to blink and miss the important moments in my life because I was too busy.

I encourage you to take stock and think about how you might live and work differently moving forward.

Starting today, how will you slow down and begin living life in real time through implementing some of the best practices shared in this chapter?

CHAPTER 10

Best Practices for Seeking Feedback

Average players want to be left alone. Good players want to be coached. Great players want to be told the truth.
Doc Rivers, NBA Coach and Former Player

When I was in the early years of my career, I recall frequently asking my bosses and co-workers, "Am I doing OK?" and "Do you have any advice for me?" in an effort to improve and accelerate my career. The generic feedback and accolades I typically received were rarely helpful and often frustrating; I yearned for something more candid and substantial to assist in my professional growth. This continued until one boss/mentor of mine challenged me to change *how* I was asking for feedback in order to get the input I desired and needed. His timely and helpful advice, which I have utilized for decades, is the basis for much of what you will read in this chapter.

As much as I personally value feedback, I have observed over most of my career that the idea of asking for feedback is difficult for some. The act of asking for candid feedback can indeed be one of the scariest things we do as professionals, but it does not have to be this way. We may fear the comments will be painful or our flaws will be exposed. Instead, I suggest we reframe our thinking to consider that the feedback we receive from colleagues and clients can help us adjust our approach, fix major issues before they get out of control, or stay the course. Feedback can and should be considered a *gift*, not something to avoid.

Here are **seven best practices** for gathering critical feedback:

1. **Make it timely.** Ask for private feedback soon after the event/issue/conversation occurred. Don't wait too long!
2. **Gather the feedback in person.** Ask for feedback in person if at all possible. Virtually or via a phone call are acceptable, but not as effective as in-person. Do not ask for feedback in an email or by sending a survey.
3. **Be a continuous learner.** Remember to approach your overall role as one of a *continuous learner*. This attitude will set you up to welcome the feedback process with open arms. We all have skills, behaviors, or technical expertise we can improve.
4. **Avoid defensiveness.** Listen carefully to the feedback and consider the possible truth in what you are hearing. Avoid appearing defensive at all costs. This will require vulnerability and humility on your part as well as some degree of self-control.
5. **Clarify.** Clarify what you're hearing. If you're not sure, ask for specific examples or clarification that will help you understand the feedback you're receiving.
6. **Be specific.** Always be specific when asking for feedback.

For example: "I think I could have done a better job presenting in our staff meeting yesterday. Do you have tips for how I can improve?" Specific questions like this will typically receive a substantive answer you can use versus a perfunctory "yes," "no," or "you are amazing!"

7. **Thank the giver.** It takes courage to speak candidly about difficult topics, and you want the person that gave the feedback to feel comfortable doing it again in the future. Remember, without feedback, we operate in a vacuum and restrict our own growth and development.

There is perhaps an eighth best practice we should consider: **Give permission to be candid**. I occasionally observe that asking someone for feedback is met with blank stares or surface accolades from the other person, which is obviously not helpful. Perhaps we should simply give key stakeholders in our work (and personal) circles *permission* to speak openly and candidly if they have something to say. Repeatedly giving this permission to be candid may eventually unlock useful feedback we can use and help the giver overcome any potential intimidation or discomfort they may be experiencing.

Another aspect of seeking feedback is accurately identifying our audience. We often gravitate to friends and colleagues we like, who rarely say anything critical. To truly benefit from a candid feedback conversation, seek out people directly affected by your work who are not close personal friends or who have a reputation for being direct. The goal of seeking candid feedback should not be accolades and validation, but genuine opportunities for learning and growth.

Once you receive the feedback, consider these next steps:

- Review everything you've heard and identify the changes you can make immediately.
- Identify the changes that may require more time or additional help and develop a step-by-step strategy to put them into action.
- Request time for another conversation with the feedback provider(s) in the coming weeks or months to assess your progress. This will help keep you accountable for applying the changes.

The helpful and candid feedback I have received over the years has been sometimes painful to hear—but ultimately transformative in my professional and personal development. I encourage you to put these best practices to work and notice the impact these feedback discussions have on the way you approach every aspect of your work and life.

What is the most helpful feedback you've received over the course of your life? What difference did it make in either your personal life or your career? How will you be more intentional about seeking feedback from others, beginning this week?

CHAPTER 11

Fixing Dysfunctional Business Meetings

Meetings are notoriously one of organizational life's most insufferable realities. U.S. companies spend more than $37 billion a year on them. Employees in American companies spend more than one-third of their time in them. And 71% of senior managers view them as unproductive.

Ron Carucci, *Harvard Business Review*

Let's admit it: If given a choice, we would likely opt for dental surgery over some of the work meetings we are forced to attend each week. I have listened to my business clients express their frustration about meetings for more than two decades. Here is a brief sampling of comments I have heard:

- "We rarely have an agenda and if we do, we don't stick to it."
- "We dance around hard topics and avoid confrontation. There is no real honesty and candid feedback is nonexistent."
- "We have meetings to plan meetings . . . to plan meetings. Drives me crazy!"

- "We often leave confused about who has responsibility for carrying out what we discussed."
- "There is little or no accountability."
- "Half the meetings I attend are unnecessary—an email would have sufficed."
- "There is no engagement or real discussion. We just review boring slide decks."
- "The Type As dominate, and nobody else gets to contribute."
- "I can't believe we don't assign someone to take notes in our meetings to be distributed to all attendees. This is why we have no accountability or alignment about what was said!"

When I probe for the reasons behind comments like these, I typically hear:

- **Status quo**—"That is just the way we have always done meetings."
- **Training**—"I don't know another way to do it. This is how I was taught."
- **Leadership**—"My boss is not interested in changing and is not very good at managing our meetings or time in general."
- **Politics and self-protective behavior**—"Nobody want to take the risk of being held closely accountable for results, so they avoid saying anything that sheds a negative light on their performance."
- **Misperceptions about candor**—"We are afraid of candid discussions about performance in our meetings. We struggle to give and receive feedback because it is always seen as negative."

If these frustrations and their causes resonate with you and you desire change, I would like to offer a list of basic best practices to help get "meeting madness" under control, improve meeting effectiveness, and create greater accountability. These suggestions apply to both meeting leaders (which can be any of us) and meeting participants who are willing to speak up for a different approach (which should be all of us).

Meeting Best Practices

- **Do we even need to have this meeting?** This is perhaps the first and most important question to ask. Can you get what you need without appropriating sixty minutes of my team's valuable time? Would emails or a few phone calls achieve the same objective? Don't be afraid to respectfully ask for the purpose of a meeting you are invited to and push back on attending if you feel it is unnecessary. Be tactful, but question whether it is the best use of your time.

- **Is there a clear agenda?** Don't try to lead or even attend a meeting without a clear agenda, preferably communicated to everyone in advance. A lack of a clear agenda is one of the biggest contributors to dysfunctional, time-wasting meetings. Without an agenda provided in advance, people show up unprepared or underprepared.

Agenda Example:
1. Our meeting time is 9:00 to 10:15 a.m. on Thursday, July 19, via Zoom (link will be shared before the meeting).
2. Our main objective is to assign responsibilities and specific deadlines for completing the ABC project.

3. Expect to participate in a short brainstorming exercise on ways to maximize the success of the ABC project.
4. Be prepared to share a status report on the specific people resources your team can provide for the project. Have this ready to share with everyone via Share Screen (keep it to one page).
5. We will plan the time and agenda for our next meeting.
6. Assign specific tasks, roles, and deadlines for all work or projects discussed.

- **Start and end on time.** It is maddening to start late or go past the stated meeting time because of tardy participants, rambling discussions, or lack of focus on the main meeting objective. Those with busy schedules have little tolerance for poorly run meetings. A gatekeeper (the leader or someone else given this task) should keep the meeting on track to ensure its timely completion.
- **Assign a scribe for every meeting.** Someone must take notes in every meeting to share later with the participants, and everyone can take turns at shouldering this responsibility. Some of my clients utilize their administrative assistants for this purpose. This is a must if you want everyone aligned around the meeting discussion and expect to hold people accountable.
- **Assign a "Yoda."** I borrowed this idea from best-selling author Keith Ferrazi: "We all remember the wise Jedi Master from Star Wars. A Yoda's job is to notice and speak up when something is being left unsaid. The Yoda may

also call out anyone whose criticism is unconstructive or disrespectful. If the Yoda has not spoken up for a period of time, the leader should interrupt the meeting and ask him/her if the group is missing anything" (*Harvard Business Review*, January–February 2012). FYI, the "Yoda" should rarely be the meeting leader; everyone should take turns and share this responsibility.

- **Encourage respectful candor/feedback in all meetings.** Meeting participants need to feel empowered to speak up, share the truth, and give and receive candid feedback.

- **Require clear ownership and strict deadlines for all action items.** Nothing is more annoying than a time-consuming meeting that ends with no clear action or accountability. Action and ambiguity do not mix well. Insist on meeting participants taking clear ownership of their ideas, suggestions, and duties, and being accountable for specific dates for completion. Include these commitments in the notes recap sent to all participants. If you are the meeting leader, set the right example by publicly sharing your own commitments and deadlines.

- **Maximize meeting participation.** What do you do if few people speak up or the loudest voices tend to dominate the meeting? If your goal is engaging in real discussions on important topics, try breaking the meeting participants into teams of two or three (no bigger) and have them go to separate corners of the meeting room—or even better, other rooms or spaces nearby. *You can also do this virtually by using the chat room feature.* Give them fifteen to twenty minutes to brainstorm solutions for an important topic and report their "team" findings to the larger group upon their return. This is a great approach to engage more introverted meeting participants and usually yields useful ideas. ***Helpful Tip***: If you are the meeting leader and are doing most of the talking, rethink your approach. Share the stage, ask for input, and see your role as the "facilitator" of great conversations rather than dominating the discussion. Also, let others on your team take turns as the meeting leader with responsibility for the agenda and follow up on accountability. This will ensure better team engagement.

- **Kill (or radically reduce) the use of slide presentations.** I have a client who will only allow four slides in a meeting presentation. He instructs his team to provide the highlights of what they need to share in a compelling, memorable way with only four slides. They can bring handouts with more detailed data if necessary for the meeting participants, but they must make do with only four slides and limited time to present. This approach created a lot of anxiety at first, but now his meetings are tighter, the right information is shared, and people stay more engaged. You might also try eliminating meeting slide presentations altogether as some of my clients have done. They have never regretted their decision.

- **Change the venue.** Be open to meeting somewhere other than the usual places. Go outside, meet over coffee or lunch, or combine the meeting with a fun team-building activity. The point is that sometimes changing the meeting location can have a positive impact on the mood and engagement level of the team. Give it a try.

We all recognize the importance of meetings, and they will never go away. But what if we found ways to meet less and spend more time doing the more important work our jobs require? What if the meetings we do participate in were more effective and engaging? If you want to give your teammates and organization a great gift, invest time in rethinking your approach to meetings and be more creative. Ask for input on making improvements and quit accepting the status quo. Even if you are only a meeting participant and not leading your own meetings yet, have the courage to make helpful suggestions for minimizing the number of meetings and improving the meetings that are necessary.

This is not a definitive best practices list, but all of the ideas I have shared have been proven to work for my clients who have tried them. Remember that meetings are for creating value, not playing politics, covering your backside, or simply because "that's how we've always done things."

If you can dramatically improve "meeting madness" for your team and your organization, the applause will be *deafening*.

Based on the best practices you have just read, incorporate at least three of them into meetings you are leading this week. If you are a meeting participant, be bold and recommend these helpful ideas to your colleagues.

PART THREE

Connection and Business Relationships

CHAPTER 12

The Ripple Effect of Our Actions

*Most of us spend too much time on what is urgent
and not enough time on what is important.*

STEPHEN R. COVEY, AUTHOR OF
THE SEVEN HABITS OF HIGHLY PRODUCTIVE PEOPLE

If you are like most of the busy professionals I know, you will be facing a large pile of work in the coming week with limited time to get it all done in the confines of a typical workday. You may feel rushed, stressed, and even overwhelmed with the challenges of getting all your work tasks completed, being present for your family and friends, and taking time to recharge and regroup. *What I am describing is a daily grind that dramatically affects how we interact with others.* When we are busy, stressed, and under pressure, we may have a tendency to see our daily actions as existing in a vacuum that only involves us, our needs, and our perspectives.

If we take seriously the need to create time for ourselves to pause, reflect, catch our breath, and think before we act, we can hopefully take it one step further. We can see the importance of considering not only our own needs, wants, and perspectives, but also the needs, wants, and perspectives of those on the receiving end of our actions. If we do not show up well or if we act with frustration, anger, or concern for only our needs, we can create a *negative ripple effect* in those experiencing us throughout the day. Sometimes, not acting at all can have an adverse effect on others as well. If we create space to be more thoughtful about what we say and do, we will more carefully consider:

- How will this person react to the email or text I am about to send or the call I am about to make?
- Am I taking the time to actively listen to their perspective?
- What is going on in their world?
- What is their stress level and current workload?
- Am I being clear in what I am asking of them?
- How will my decision(s) affect the circles around me? Have I carefully considered all the positive and negative ramifications?
- If I am a leader, am I conveying hope and encouragement? Am I seizing the moment to coach someone to perform better?
- Will my actions inspire someone to be and feel better— or worse?
- Do I take the time to ask how I can help? What does this person need from me most right now?

I will be the first to admit that I sometimes fall into the trap of focusing single-mindedly on getting work off my plate and checking off items on my to-do lists, only to realize I could have done a better job of considering how I am impacting others. When I follow my own advice from chapter 11, I schedule time between meetings that allows me to prepare and be more thoughtful about the needs of the other attendees. I schedule specific time each day to get work done without distraction. With more air on my calendar, I am calmer and less stressed overall, which means I choose my words more carefully in emails or texts. I am engaged and actively listen during my phone and video call conversations.

When we consider the ripple effect that results from *all* our actions, we may be compelled to be more thoughtful and focused on those with whom we engage each day. We will stop living exclusively in our own world and start living more in theirs. What if we filtered all our actions toward others during the workday through the prism of courtesy, kindness, respect, empathy, compassion, and gratitude? Think of the positive impact we could make! We are all capable of doing more of this if we slow down enough to consider it and simply make the commitment to do it. If only one person is better off after they engage with us at the end of every day, the effort will be absolutely worth it.

What ripple effect will your actions have today?

CHAPTER 13

The Importance of RAPKG

*The ultimate test of your greatness is
the way you treat every human being.*

Pope St. John Paul II

Some time ago I received a thank-you note from someone
who had attended one of my corporate workshops on how to
maximize business relationships. The person was thoughtful
in sending the note, but I especially appreciated the specific
reference to the best practices that resonated with her and how
she planned to apply them in her life. This note of gratitude
and the lessons it contained have stuck with me and has been
the catalyst for some deeper thinking about the importance
of something the workplace and the world desperately needs:
random acts of praise, kindness, and gratitude—or "RAPKG"
for short.

I have long observed that despite the myriad ways we
are connected (in a superficial way) to one another through
technology and social media, the opportunities for genuine
and more substantive relationships are diminishing. It may be

that our interest in building stronger relationships is fading as well. It is important that we fight past this growing cultural norm, and RAPKG is a helpful way to do it. Consider the numerous opportunities we have each day to reach out to our work colleagues, clients, or extended network of friends and offer a brief message of praise for a job well done, do something kind for them, or express our gratitude for something they may have done for us. This approach costs us nothing and will help us strengthen old relationships and foster new ones. It is a worthwhile and noble practice we should all follow.

Getting Started

In order for RAPKG to thrive, we need to be *intentional, selfless, measured,* and *specific.* First, I recommend incorporating some *intentionality* into your "randomness" and put RAPKG on your calendar every Monday morning. Let this serve as a reminder to reflect on the people you encountered the previous week that you might want to reach out to with a note, call, email, or meeting request to offer praise, kindness, or gratitude. I do this weekly, and it takes less than thirty minutes. ***Helpful Tip:*** If you feel compelled to act in the moment or want to practice RAPKG sooner, don't wait for Mondays!

Second, be *selfless*; don't attach expectations to your RAPKG. Make it about others, not about you. This practice is about giving to others, so don't ever keep score. You will reap rewards down the road in unexpected and delightful ways if you look at RAPKG like dropping a pebble in a pond. The ripple effect of your selfless acts will have a positive impact on the recipient and possibly others as they begin the practice toward people in their extended circles.

Third, be *measured* in how you practice RAPKG, especially in the area of praise. Unrestrained praise given too frequently has the effect of negating the positive impact intended. If everything is praise-worthy, then nothing is praise-worthy. A measured approach to praise, when it is truly deserved, is always best. Acting in a measured way is less important for sharing kindness and gratitude; my only advice is to start small and expand your efforts gradually as you begin to cultivate this practice in your daily life. This will help you feel less overwhelmed by the daily opportunities to practice RAPKG.

Finally, be *specific* in your application of RAPKG. Don't reach out and say, "Hey, I just wanted you to know I think you are awesome!" Though well-intentioned, you will miss an opportunity with this vague message to specifically praise a behavior or action you want to encourage more of in the other person. If someone does something for which you are grateful, tell him or her exactly what it was that inspired our gratitude. ***Helpful Tip***: Specificity is not as strictly applied to our random acts of kindness, as ALL acts of kindness, no matter how small, are good. Remember that an act of kindness can also consist of candid and challenging feedback delivered in a respectful manner to a colleague or friend.

Ways to Apply RAPKG

In the weeks leading up to this book's publication, I took the time to document a few opportunities I had to apply RAPKG, which I hope will inspire creative ways for you to make this practice work in your own lives:

- I sent a note to one of my coaching clients praising her for the excellent leadership I observed in her during a meeting she led for her entire organization. She did an outstanding job that I wanted to acknowledge, and I also let her know I shared the positive feedback with her boss. *Helpful Tip*: Always keep thank-you notes on hand. They are a great way to apply RAPKG and are more meaningful than emails.

- I took time out of a particularly hectic day to have a long conversation with a security guard who works for one of my corporate clients. He told me about his upcoming weekend plans, and I asked how his family was doing. He is one of the nicest and friendliest people I have ever met. He always greets people with a smile, and I am grateful to know him. How often do we stop and invest in a conversation with the countless people from all stations in life we encounter? How often do we treat them as they deserve with courtesy, respect, and kindness? "Kind words can be short and easy to speak, but their echoes are truly endless" (St. Teresa of Calcutta).

- I had an opportunity to express gratitude to my wife for a difficult conversation she had with our youngest son. She handled it beautifully and got our son back on track. My wife was not aware I heard the conversation, but it meant a lot to her that I recognized the difficulty and thanked her.

More Examples of RAPKG

- A senior executive sent flowers and a thank-you note to the wife of one of his direct reports to express his gratitude for how she supported and encouraged her husband during an extremely difficult period for the company.

- A newly hired team member was forced to stand in for her sick boss and give a nerve-racking and difficult presentation to the senior executive team on her tenth day with the company. She received a handwritten note from the CEO that afternoon praising her effort and offering suggestions for ways to make it even better. The CEO also offered to mentor the new team member once a month and help her acclimate to the company.

- A consultant friend of mine started the practice of making donations to the favorite causes of her clients in their name at Christmas and for other special occasions (an idea I have borrowed!). Instead of the usual fruit or cookie baskets, she demonstrates her understanding of what truly matters to her clients with her kind and thoughtful gifts in their name.

Other Ideas

- Invest time in someone who is looking for a job and offer advice and access to your network.
- Give the gift of a book that had a positive effect on you to someone who would also benefit from reading it.
- Treat your team to lunch and thank them for their hard work after a difficult project.
- Offer the gift of mentorship and advice to a younger colleague and invest in their success.
- Reach out to a colleague who is experiencing difficulties outside of work and offer them encouragement and a listening ear.

- Practice gratitude in every area of your life. "Cultivate the habit of being grateful for every good thing that comes to you, and to give thanks continuously. And because all things have contributed to your advancement, you should include all things in your gratitude" (Ralph Waldo Emerson).

I would love to tell you that I have RAPKG all figured out, but I do not. I likely miss a significant number of opportunities each week to practice it, but I am sincerely trying to improve, and I feel that I am making progress. Any effort in this area will have a positive impact on others and contribute to my personal and professional growth, and that makes RAPKG even more worthwhile.

The Fruits of RAPKG

The pay-it-forward ripple effect of practicing RAPKG is obvious, but there are other fruits to be had from putting this into practice. Here are a few:

- **Improves the quality of your relationships.** If you are interested in finding meaningful ways to actively engage with your business network outside of the usual agenda, this is an excellent option. The quality of these relationships will grow as a result of your thoughtful outreach. RAPKG removes barriers and fosters trust.
- **Allows you to join the ranks of the exceptional.** The men and women I have encountered over the years who actively and quietly engage in RAPKG are often recognized as exceptional leaders within their organizations.

- **Overcomes division.** Much of the division and animosity in our society often spills over into the workplace, forcing us into cliques or silos. Practicing random acts of praise, kindness, and gratitude, if done well, transcends division and is indifferent to political affiliation, race, religious preferences, titles, sexual orientation, or socioeconomic backgrounds.

RAPKG is not another company program or "flavor of the month" concept. This is about reaching out in a positive way with a different mindset to the people we encounter every day in work and life. We control this mindset, and there are no barriers or limits except the ones we create for ourselves. In addition to the numerous reasons I have shared about why RAPKG is important, it is simply the right thing to do. The workplace and the world could be transformed through more random acts of praise, kindness, and gratitude if you and I have the courage to positively change how we engage with those around us.

Who will be the beneficiary of your RAPKG today?

CHAPTER 14

Storytelling for Leaders

Over the years I have become convinced that we learn best—and change—from hearing stories that strike a chord within us… Those in leadership positions who fail to grasp or use the power of stories risk failure for their companies and for themselves.

JOHN KOTTER, HARVARD BUSINESS SCHOOL PROFESSOR AND AUTHOR OF *LEADING CHANGE*

I vividly recall a visit a few years ago from my father a few days after his eighty-first birthday. Reaching one's early eighties in fairly good health is quite an achievement in itself, but what dawned on me during this special visit was the richness of my dad's life as he shared with his grandsons stories of his past. I appreciated that he shared not only the fun and happy stories, but the adversity and heartbreak he has faced as well. My father long ago realized that one of the few treasures he has left to give us are the stories and experiences from his life. I never fail to glean something valuable from this man I know so well, and my sons never tire of listening to their Papa.

Shortly after my father's visit, I drove to meet a friend for coffee. My friend is a respected senior business leader with responsibility for a large organization, and he shared with me that a few of his direct reports were struggling with performance issues, and his overall organization was coming off a poor quarter. With my dad's visit fresh in my mind, after listening to the myriad reasons why he thought his team was struggling, I felt compelled to ask a simple question: "How often do you reflect on your personal business successes and failures with your team and share the detailed lessons with them?"

His blank stare spoke volumes. As we continued our conversation, he admitted with some embarrassment that reflection and sharing were not easy for him. His mindset regarding his team had long been "I've done it, and so can you. You are all smart and will figure it out, just like I did." He also told me he had little time to invest in his team because of the hectic schedule he typically keeps. Based on my experience and countless other conversations with leaders, this problem is fairly pervasive in business today. Those of us who are senior leaders are often so busy chasing the "numbers" or tackling the latest business challenge that we may be leaving our less experienced colleagues to struggle on their own rather than making the time investment required to help them succeed. We may fail to recognize the positive power of storytelling in coaching our teams to success—and the thought of revealing our struggles in front of others may trigger irrational fears.

Four Helpful Ideas for Business Leaders

1. **Recognize the power of personal example and your own story.** Share your business successes and failures with the team; tell them what you learned and how you improved over time. Dedicate a portion of your

team meetings or one-on-one conversations to be a true teacher who is willing to share relevant business successes, failures, and lessons from your past—not just holding them accountable for the end result.

2. **Break it down.** What you think is trivial may be important and helpful to someone without your depth of experience. I strongly suggest starting with the outcome of a past deal, project, or business situation (successful or not), and work your way backward to the very beginning. Give them all the steps and your lessons learned. Be humble enough to admit and own your mistakes.

3. **Be a mentor (as someone once was for you).** You have done well and been promoted for your hard work and your track record of success. Congratulations! Did someone help you along the way? Did you have a mentor or internal advocate to guide you on the journey? As leaders, we all have a responsibility to mentor, coach, and develop those in our charge and share our experiences and hard-fought wisdom with them. This will take a time investment you may believe you don't have, but the ramifications of *not* developing your people can be seen in high attrition, poor performance, and missed goals. You have many priorities, but this should make your Top 5 list every week.

4. **Be aware that your experiences are not necessarily their experiences.** If you want the team to follow your example and emulate your success, be open and honest about the challenges they face. Listen to them. Humbly let

them know about your own struggles. Their experiences and backgrounds may be very different from your own, and each generation learns and develops in a different way. Data suggests that Millennials and Generation Zers desire to know the "why" of what they are being asked to do. Adapt and be flexible with your approach and give them what they are seeking (and desperately need) from you.

If this chapter resonates with you and you desire to make changes, the path forward is simple. Be more intentional about making time for your team each week, candidly share your detailed stories (successes and failures), don't assume anything, and meet them where they are (not where you think they should be based on *your* experiences). They need the tactics, not just the strategy. Some will get it faster than others, but good leaders should desire success that is broadly sustainable and not just driven by a few superstars.

My father's visit reminded me of the power of storytelling, and I am grateful for his gift. There is a great mentor, coach, and storyteller inside each of you with countless lessons to share. Be wise and let your team learn from your struggles and successes.

Everybody will win when you do.

Look for opportunities this week to share one of your personal stories with someone who needs to hear it.

CHAPTER 15

Essential Lessons for Better Business Relationships

Living a connected life leads one to take a different view. Life is less a quest than a quilt. We find meaning, love, and prosperity through the process of stitching together our bold attempts to help others find their own way in their lives. The relationships we weave become an exquisite and endless pattern.

KEITH FERRAZZI, AUTHOR OF *NEVER EAT ALONE: AND OTHER SECRETS TO SUCCESS, ONE RELATIONSHIP AT A TIME*

I have long been a keen student of the *essential tactics* and *simple engagement approaches* that are critical for building effective business relationships both inside and outside our organizations. Nothing gets better simply because we wish it, and this certainly applies to how we approach relationships in the business world. There are no magic answers and few shortcuts to being great at relationship building. Improvement takes hard work, self-discipline, intentionality, and commitment. It takes a willingness to change old habits and develop new approaches. Also, it takes the recognition that sometimes focusing on the basics and embracing simplicity often work best.

Essential Tactics

Here are **ten essential tactics** I have found to be the most consistently helpful in successfully forging effective business relationships over my career:

1. **Embrace your personality style.** I have known for decades that I am a high-functioning introvert. Instead of following conventional wisdom and attending countless anxiety-producing networking events, I have long pursued a one-on-one approach to meeting new people as well as meeting my existing network over coffee or lunch where I am more comfortable. I also try to end my meetings by 4:30 p.m. each day and get back to my home office to write, catch up on administrative work, exercise, and savor the alone time I need each day before engaging with my family.

2. **Leverage LinkedIn.** I have a simple rule: Everyone I encounter in person or by phone receives an invitation (*always* with a personal note providing context) to join my LinkedIn network within twenty-four hours of contact. This self-discipline helps me continuously add to my network with business professionals I encounter. LinkedIn provides a well-organized and convenient way to keep track of your network and provides easy access to their background information. The LinkedIn app is especially helpful when you need quick access to background information on your phone about someone you are meeting.

3. **Nurture the network.** Nurture existing relationships at the same time you are expanding new ones. Much

like a garden, healthy relationships must be maintained, and this takes work. The worst thing we can do is reach out to someone in our hour of need and realize that we failed to maintain the relationship. I keep a spreadsheet with every client, prospect, and business friend alphabetically listed with contact information and a section for notes. This helps me keep track of my large network, stay on top of required follow-up and future meetings I need to schedule,

4. **Put everything on the calendar.** Everything important in your life is likely scheduled, right? Why not treat your approach to business relationships the same way? My meetings, reminders about the topics of upcoming discussions, follow-up items, birthdays, anniversaries, etc., are all part of my calendar.

5. **Rethink how you spend your time.** If you see little time for building business relationships on your busy calendar, let me challenge you a bit. There are five opportunities a week for coffee or breakfast, five opportunities a week for lunch, and five opportunities for dinner. Start utilizing at least three or four of these fifteen opportunities each week to meet with someone new (or nurture an existing business relationship). You have to eat, so why not spend this time with another professional and accomplish two objectives during this time?

6. **Make it easy for them (not you).** When you are in "exploring" mode with a new business contact, if you make the meeting time and venue as convenient as humanly possible for them, they are more likely to

attend. This may mean before work, at lunch, or after work. In my experience, early coffee near their office is almost always the most convenient time and place. Your convenience is *not* as important as theirs in the early phases of relationship building.

7. **Embrace the basics.** Always be courteous. Always be grateful. Acknowledge that you know the other person is investing valuable time in meeting you and you appreciate this. The basics always work, and this is as basic as it gets! Follow up in a timely manner with a thank-you note (an email is okay, but not as memorable).

8. **Focus on relationships, not acquaintances.** Meeting someone only once makes them an acquaintance, at best, *not* a relationship. You have to invest energy and thought into having multiple meetings you both see as beneficial. This is one of the reasons I cringe at the thought of collecting fifty business cards at networking events.

9. **Be personal.** Meeting someone for the first time? Not sure what to say? Do you desire a meaningful conversation about real issues and not the usual surface or politically correct dialogue? Be transparent first. Get personal (with discernment). Be authentic. If you desire someone to open up to you, you should be open about your life first. In effect, this gives the other person "permission" to be open about topics outside of work if you take the first step in sharing.

10. **Always make "deposits."** I encourage my clients to view their business networks as a "relationship economy." In this economy, you should be consistently

offering to help and investing in the people in your business network (making deposits). A day will come when you may be in need of help, a favor, or maybe just a listening ear, and you will have an easier time making a "withdrawal" if you have been making deposits along the way.

A Simple Three-Step Approach to Engagement

Before my father retired, he was a master of building business relationships and was well-respected and trusted by all who knew him throughout his long career. I remember well the advice he gave me many years ago when I graduated from the University of Georgia and was about to begin my own business career. He told me to think about three basic approaches when I was encountering new professionals as I began my first post-college job:

1. Be helpful; serve their needs.
2. Be sincerely curious.
3. Always add value.

It took me a few years to fully grasp the importance of what he told me, but his sage advice is at the core of how I have approached my relationships over the course of my career. Here is what my father's simple wisdom has come to mean to me today.

Be helpful; serve their needs—My father's first tip was to approach everyone with a servant's heart. My parents were servant leaders throughout their lives, so I was fortunate to have this behavior modeled for me from a very young age. When you make your efforts about sincerely helping others and serving their needs, you will find relationship building to be a worthwhile, fulfilling experience that will ultimately come back to you in positive and unexpected ways. When it is all about you and your needs, people see through that, and your attempts at relationship building can become a miserable, laborious experience on many levels. Sincerely ask, "Is there anything I can do to help you?" or simply do something for them out of generosity with no expectation of return. As my father used to say, "Always make it about them, not about you."

Be sincerely curious—My father's second tip stemmed from his understanding that meeting a lot of senior businesspeople as a new professional might make me feel intimidated and nervous. He encouraged me to be genuinely curious about others as a helpful way to counter my lack of experience and my misguided view that I needed to have all the answers. I have learned from experience that people find us more interesting when we ask them questions. I have also learned that people appreciate when someone genuinely wishes to learn something new or just desires to know them better. In the early years of my career, I would typically go to meetings with interesting and thoughtful questions prepared in advance. Years later, I am able to recall from experience the most appropriate questions to ask in most situations. Being curious takes the pressure off and stimulates a more engaging and balanced conversation.

Always add value—My dad's final tip was a little difficult for me to understand when I was twenty-one, and it took me a few years to finally get it. He encouraged me to always approach every meeting with the mindset that I owned the responsibility for the other person to feel the meeting was well worth their time. He encouraged me to find ways to add value to every conversation or meeting. Today, this concept of adding value takes many forms: being a good listener, offering helpful advice, making a connection to someone in my network, giving the gift of a book, or following up with a helpful article related to our conversation. This particular tip, when practiced well, almost always generates numerous follow-up meetings that lead to strong relationships and even close friendships.

This simple approach to engagement and the "essential tactics" I shared earlier have proven to be invaluable in my desire to build authentic business relationships. These concepts work well with internal company relationships as well as with those outside your organization. Don't overcomplicate or add unnecessary layers to relationship building. Develop a simple and actionable approach that works for you. Just be yourself, be helpful, be curious, and add value while utilizing the tactics I have shared. I promise this ongoing investment in relationship building will be one of the most rewarding and satisfying efforts of your career.

Pick one of the essential tactics and make it your focus this week. Evaluate the impact this has on your relationships and then pick another to focus on the following week. Keep doing this until you have tried them all.

CHAPTER 16

Cultivating the Curiosity Skill Set

The greatest compliment that was ever paid me was when someone asked me what I thought and attended to my answer.

HENRY DAVID THOREAU

Curiosity is one of my favorite skills and one I have worked hard to develop ever since I was a new professional just out of college. I love to ask questions and learn about people's lives, interests, challenges, and successes, and I am always willing to be transparent and share about my life as well. I have long realized that when you're genuinely curious, you must actively listen to the other person. Nothing builds trust and deepens relationships more effectively than allowing another person to feel truly listened to and valued. I am also a strong advocate for getting to know both the personal and work aspects of someone's life, with a preference for the personal side first.

Forging New Relationships

An effective starting point for all relationships is building empathy—stepping into the other person's shoes and seeing the world through their eyes. We accomplish this by breaking down walls and building rapport through genuine curiosity. Here are some of my favorite questions when I meet someone new in both personal and work settings:

- "What sort of work do you do?"
- "Did you do anything fun this past weekend?
- "What are your plans this coming weekend?"
- "When you are not working, where do you like to invest your time and energy?"
- "This has been an interesting year filled with challenges and surprises. What are you doing to deal with everything personally and professionally?"

Notice that none of these questions will solicit simple yes or no answers; instead, they require responses that will give you helpful insights into who the person is and what is interesting and important to them. After carefully *listening* to their answers, you will find that you can highlight shared experiences and introduce additional questions informed by what you just learned about them:

- "That is very interesting. I used to be a runner as well. Do you run any competitive races? What else do you do to stay fit?"
- "That sounds like a great trip. My family loves to travel as well. What are some of your favorite destinations?"
- "I agree. It has been an interesting year for us as well. You mentioned job stress . . . what sort of work do you do?"

When we encounter new people, we utilize the skill of curiosity to learn more about them and to find areas of similarity or shared interests. By asking people questions, we also have an opportunity to show genuine **interest and respect.** We should always try to balance seeking information about them with sharing information about ourselves. A good conversation is not a monologue, but rather an exchange in which two people are genuinely engaged, listening, responding, and connecting to each other. In fact, our willingness to share a little about ourselves *first* can often be a helpful way to encourage the other person to share as well in response to our questions. Recognize that authenticity is also greatly enhanced by mutual sharing— and sharing thrives in an atmosphere of curiosity.

Here are two examples:

- "My wife and I had a really full weekend with the kids. With the kids' sports activities, yard projects, and church, we had a lot going on. How was your weekend?"
- "Working from home has posed some interesting challenges for me, and I am still trying to figure it out. Do you work from home? Can you share any insights with me about how to be more effective from a home office?"

Positioning the question after you share first can elicit a deeper response from the other person and encourage them to give more substantive answers. Also, this approach gives the other person complete freedom and discretion to share as much or little information as they choose. Going deeper is always better in my opinion, but not everyone is ready to share as much as you, and that is perfectly fine. Be respectful. Be patient.

Curiosity at Work

I observe that leaders and other professionals in my network often overlook the value of curiosity in work conversations. Curiosity at work will help you transform "work colleagues" into valuable and mutually beneficial professional relationships, as well as foster greater engagement. We are typically so busy that we may feel there isn't enough time to invest in a conversation that deviates from the business at hand. What a missed opportunity! We often fail to learn about how our colleagues are really doing, what they are feeling, and how they are experiencing life in general. We may end up getting perfunctory answers to our work questions instead of the more honest and open discussions we crave.

The answer might be more patience and better listening on our part. Perhaps we should meet our team members and colleagues where they are and invest in getting to know more about their interests and lives outside of work. We may need to simply ask their opinions with a sincere desire to hear their thoughts . . . and just absorb what they say without judgment. By the way, this investment in curiosity, listening, and discussing the personal side of life builds *trust*, which is also an essential building block of strong business relationships.

Curiosity to Improve Engagement and Performance

I can't think of a single business leader who would not benefit from demonstrating more curiosity at work. We often miss opportunities for candid and substantive conversations because we fail to ask questions and show genuine curiosity. Asking probing questions of others rather than merely stating our opinions can often provide an opportunity to bring difficult topics to light, drive better results with our team members, and help us improve our own performance. Examples can look like this:

- "Mike, do you feel like you are having the kind of success you envisioned in your new role?"
- "Sarah, I am concerned that you might miss your goals this quarter. What do you see as the obstacles in your way and how can I help you overcome them? "

Here are some other examples of powerful questions:

- "I am new to my role. Do you have specific coaching tips for me on how I can be successful?"
- "Can you help me understand . . . ?"
- "What is something you are working on that you are excited about?"
- "I don't think I did a very good job presenting yesterday. Do you have specific tips on how I can improve my content and presenting style?"
- "What are at least three obstacles holding us back from the success we want?"
- "What are we doing right now as a team that is working well?"
- "What do you need most from me right now?"

It goes without saying that there are obligations associated with these kinds of questions. We have a responsibility to help people feel safe and comfortable in sharing what they really think. We have an obligation to actively listen and demonstrate that we've clearly heard them. We have a responsibility to follow up, explore further, and hold them and ourselves accountable to any specific commitments made in these conversations. If curiosity is going to thrive and we desire to grow this skill, we have to practice it and follow through when we utilize it.

Curiosity to Strengthen Personal Connections at Work

Take the time to invest in meeting people where they are and be patient, as it may take a while for them to trust and feel comfortable opening up. Be intentional about scheduling one-on-one conversations with colleagues where work is only a sliver of the agenda and the rest is good old-fashioned conversation filled with life, family, struggles, successes, and hopefully a little humor. Ask questions with an authentic desire to learn about the other person. Three of my favorite questions I use with coaching clients at the beginning of a conversation are: "Can we talk about life outside of work for a few minutes before we jump into business? How is life treating you? How is your family?" Show sincere interest. Actively listen. Take notes to demonstrate the importance of what is being discussed. Be empathetic.

Commit to being insatiably curious about others. Learn and remember personal things about others such as their spouse's and kids' names, hobbies, interests, and birthdays. Remember that people find you more interesting when you ask questions. Stuck on knowing the perfect thing to say? *Ask questions.* Want to make a favorable impression on a colleague, key stakeholder, manager, or others in your network and learn important information about them? *Ask questions.* Want to transform your work acquaintances into solid relationships? *Ask questions.*

Six Best Practices for Fostering Curiosity

I am a keen observer of people and am always interested in gathering best practices for personal and professional growth I can use and share with others. It is my belief that curiosity is a competency that can be cultivated and developed like any other. As I reflect on people in my network who excel at curiosity, these are behaviors and mindsets I believe they consistently exhibit to foster this valuable skill:

1. **It's not all about me.** People who are great at curiosity understand that we can't focus only on our own agendas, needs, and interests. They recognize what a turnoff it is for others when we make the conversation all about us, and instead they always strive for truly two-way conversations.

2. **Willingness to learn.** Genuinely curious people have a strong desire to learn and ask questions to enrich their understanding, acquire knowledge, and grow. We model curiosity for those around us when we show a willingness to ask questions and humbly admit we don't always know the answer.

3. **We don't need to be in control.** Effective curiosity is about being comfortable with the unknown. It's OK to not know how the conversation will turn out and take a leap of faith that it will unfold as it should without micromanaging or forcing our preferred outcome.

4. **Understanding the danger of certainty.** Certainty is when we are convinced that our opinions are definitely true. This may be rooted to some degree in ego or arrogance. This can lead to incorrect assumptions about others and having a closed mind when engaging in conversation. It can also lead us to choke off dialogue by trying to solve every problem because we are convinced we have the answers. Curiosity is often an effective antidote to certainty.

5. **It's a human thing.** We humans desire connection and relationship, even if we would describe ourselves as having shy or introverted personalities. Curiosity provides the catalyst for transforming boring or one-sided conversations into opportunities for greater engagement and hopefully stronger relationships.

6. **Promote psychological safety.** People who are the most effective practitioners of curiosity are excellent at making people feel safe and comfortable (with zero repercussions) about honestly speaking their minds, sharing ideas, pointing out problems, and sharing personal aspects of their lives (even their personal struggles).

I have learned from my parents, mentors, and other leaders I have worked with over the course of my career that curiosity is an invaluable skill that we all can and should more fully develop. Curiosity is the essential catalyst for building relationships, increasing engagement with colleagues, and improving our performance as well as the performance of our work colleagues. It helps us learn and enrich our lives by inviting others to share their wisdom with us. Reflect on this final thought: The next time you are in a conversation with anyone, remember that we would all be better served to do *less telling* and *more asking*.

How will you grow your curiosity skills based on what you learned in this chapter, beginning tomorrow?

CHAPTER 17

Time Is a Gift

Dost thou love life? Then do not squander time,
for that is the stuff life is made of.

BENJAMIN FRANKLIN

Time is a finite resource and we only have so much of it to harness and share. As I encounter other busy professionals, I am always struck by the common struggle we all have when it comes to finding enough time for work, family, friends, relaxation . . . you get the picture. Learning how to share time wisely is also about having our priorities in order. I recall a relevant story a client of mine shared with me about his five-year-old daughter and a conversation they had on the topic of time. He had been traveling constantly for work over the last several years and had missed a lot of family time. Feeling guilty, he had always tried to take his family on big vacations every year to fun destinations around the world as a way of making up for missed time at home. When he shared the plans for one such vacation trip with his young daughter, she responded not with excitement as he expected, but with a sigh and a sad face.

When he asked what was wrong, she replied: "Daddy, can we just read a book together? I don't care about the trip. I just want to be with you."

After my client shared this story with tears in his eyes, he walked me through all the changes he planned to make to his travel schedule to spend more time with his family. He recognized that his priorities were out of whack and that he had a distorted view of how and where to invest his time. How do you consider the topic of time? Do you have stories like the one my client shared?

In this chapter, I would like to narrowly explore time as a gift, applied through a spirit of generosity. If we look at our time as a gift to share and not simply a resource to manage, we open up possibilities for transforming time into something more noble and worthwhile. Acting with generosity . . . seeing our time is a gift . . . creating something more noble—*think about the positive difference we could make in the world if we all thought this way.*

In my opinion, there are **four primary beneficiaries** of your gifts of time:

1. **Yourself.** Yes, time can be a gift you give yourself. There is an ever-growing need for all of us to practice better self-care and invest in addressing our physical, mental, emotional, and spiritual needs. Remember, when the plane is going down, you should always put on your own oxygen mask first.

2. **Your family, friends, and neighbors.** Every precious and distraction-free minute I spend with my wife and children is a priceless and irreplaceable investment in

our family's well-being. Investing time in my friends, neighbors, and extended family helps me stay plugged into a larger world of meaningful relationships that enriches me beyond measure.

3. **Your work colleagues.** A struggling co-worker, a younger colleague in need of development, or a team in need of your energy, idea, or expertise can all benefit from the gift of your time. Instead of looking at your busy daily work calendar as a nuisance, look at each scheduled hour as a way to generously invest your time in the service of your fellow team members.

4. **Your community and great causes.** Rather than allowing your generosity to be restricted to online donations, how might you give more of yourself (and your time) to your local community, your faith community or the nonprofits you support? How can you show up and involve your family and friends in your efforts as well? Is there a job seeker who needs your help? A student you can mentor?

As you read this, I encourage you to look at the various roles and responsibilities you have as wonderful opportunities to be generous and share your time. I see the responsibilities from my own numerous roles as blessings, not burdens; they are valuable ways to connect with people I care about and truly wish to serve. In my experience, every investment of time we make signals to the recipient that they are *important*. They *matter*. They are worth the time and are *valued*.

The best way you can help, serve, and enrich relationships with the people in your life is to be fully present and make quality time for them. This is one of the most valuable gifts you can share, and I hope you will discover new ways to offer your time in the years to come.

By the way, the story I shared earlier about my client happened three years ago. He did reduce his travel considerably, while still doing a great job for his company. He changed his priorities and how he viewed time. He now understands his time investment in his family is a precious gift that he is grateful he can provide. *And he reads books with his daughter every chance he gets.*

How will you share the gift of your time today?

PART FOUR

What's It All For?

CHAPTER 18

Personal Mission Statements and Leading a Meaningful Life

The two most important days of your life are the day that you're born and the day that you find out why.

MARK TWAIN

I vividly recall a meeting several years ago with one of my executive coaching clients, someone I would describe as an intense person who had so much energy she would make coffee nervous. About two weeks into our working relationship, she walked into the room, obviously very excited to share something with me. She placed a two-page document on the table between us and declared: "I want to discuss mission statements today!" She then asked me to share my own mission statement before we discussed hers. She eagerly took out her notebook to write down what she assumed would be a lengthy description of my own mission statement. "It is only two words, so there is no need to take notes," I said, much to her bewilderment.

"How can that be? There's no way your mission statement is only two words!"

I smiled at her and said, "If you will let me finish, I will tell you. My mission statement is simple: "Serve others.""

Now she was totally flabbergasted. "I just don't see how that can be your mission statement. Mine is almost two pages!"

"Well, when I was in my twenties and thirties, I probably had something that looked like yours. But as I have grown older, I have embraced simplicity, and I've come to realize that I get everything I need in this life by putting others before myself. I learned this lesson from my parents, countless life experiences, and my faith. By serving the needs of others, I make a living and support my family through my coaching, consulting, books, and speaking. I am part of a worthwhile mission by helping others achieve their full potential. My company is called Serviam Partners for a reason—*Serviam* is Latin for 'I Will Serve.' I love what I do and feel very fortunate that my work and mission are so aligned."

She was speechless as she took all this in. We carefully reviewed her two-page mission statement and eventually pared it down to two sentences. Much of it sounded like a master's thesis in college, so we removed the unnecessary and superfluous language. My client gained greater clarity and focus with a simple, more focused version of what her mission was meant to be. Whenever we touch base all these years later, we always talk about this mission statement conversation, and she has frequently encouraged me to share the story with others.

What Is Your Mission Statement?

Many of the leaders I have encountered over the years struggle to answer this question. They are often successful by the world's standards, but they feel strongly that something important is missing in their lives, and they lack direction and purpose. If compelled to come up with something, they typically offer some kind of a rambling, lengthy version.

Mission statements should be *clarifying, aspirational,* and *actionable.* In my opinion, the most meaningful mission statements are connected to giving and are lived in the service of others. They are *not* created for show, but rather have deep personal meaning. As each day begins, all of us should know with every fiber of our being what our own mission is and how we will integrate our actions and words into making it come to life. Your mission statement will ultimately serve as a guideline for all your habits, routines, decisions, and future goals.

Here are a few relevant examples:

- **If the mission is to be the best mom or dad you can be**, go to your workplace determined to do excellent work to financially support your family. Be clear about your boundaries and strive for better work/life balance. When spending time with the family, give them your full attention and avoid distractions. Make work serve your family, instead of having them serve your work.

- **If the mission is to serve your community and great causes**, consider each day how to utilize your influence in getting your company, work colleagues, and extended network to support the community in which you work and the causes that matter to you. Because I have a son with autism, I have never hesitated to promote autism awareness and enlist support for helping people on the autism spectrum from my work colleagues and friends.

- **If the mission is simply to be happy,** carefully consider those actions, experiences, and people that bring you happiness and strive to spend as much time doing these things with this group of people as often as you can. Also consider that igniting happiness in others is another way to fulfill this mission.

If you are looking for practical steps on how to get started in defining your mission statement, try these **four key steps**:

1. **Make a list of your core values.** What are the principles by which you wish to live each day? Where do your values come from? How do you think and act from a values-inspired perspective every day? Revisit the first chapter's deep dive into our need for a moral compass.
2. **Make a list of your skills and talents.** What are you good at? What can you offer to others?
3. **Make a list of everything you care about.** Family? Friends? Community? Excelling at your career? Learning new skills?
4. **Boil it down to something simple.** What is the *simplest* way possible to live out your values and maximize your skills and talents in order to facilitate greater happiness and a sense of mission? In my case, this exercise led me to understand that a *determined focus on serving others* was the most effective way to serve God, my family, friends, clients, and community and live out my values. This service brings me fulfillment and joy and permeates everything I attempt to do each day.

I wrote this chapter because knowing *who you are* and *what you are called to do* is a critical component of living a more meaningful life—and a strong personal mission statement can help you get there. It is important to realize that mission statements can and should evolve and change over time. My mission statement at age thirty-two is vastly different from the mission statement I now have in my fifties. As a young adult, I was focused on climbing the corporate ladder as fast as possible with little understanding of what I would do if and when I reached the top. After a twenty-five-year career in corporate America, I launched Serviam Partners in 2013. One of the primary motivators for starting the company was my desire to fulfill my mission of serving others more intentionally in all areas of my professional and personal life.

Probably the greatest revelation for me over the years has been the sense of peace and joy I feel that comes from helping and serving other people. I work every day through my coaching, consulting, books, and speaking engagements to influence positive outcomes for the people I encounter in my life. I make a lot of mistakes, and I certainly don't have all the answers, but I am clear about my goals and my desire to take the right approach in the service of others. The path to get here has had many twists and turns, but I am grateful for the countless lessons I've learned on this journey.

I encourage you to reflect carefully today on this idea of a personal mission statement. If you have one, kudos to you! If not, I hope this chapter will be a source of encouragement and help you develop one for yourself. It has made a tremendous difference in my life, and I believe it will in yours as well.

ESSENTIAL WISDOM

Reflect on what you have just read. If you don't have a clear and actionable mission statement, plan to create one today. If you do have one, take some time to review and refine it.

CHAPTER 19

Facing Veracruz Moments

*Most people fail not because of a lack of desire
but because of a lack of commitment.*

Vince Lombardi, Legendary NFL Coach and Hall of Famer

As you may recall from history, the Spanish conquistador Hernan Cortes and his small army of 600 men landed in Veracruz, Mexico, in 1519 with dreams of conquering the mighty Aztec empire. Many of his men were afraid and filled with doubts in the face of such a daunting mission, so Cortes made the decision to *burn their ships*. With retreat now impossible and no place to go except forward to face their enemy, his men were properly motivated and fully committed to fulfill their mission.

Many of my clients deal with the challenge of commitment, and I have certainly had my own numerous encounters with it over my career. Being fully committed means being "all in" and can include the way we approach big strategic decisions, how much effort we are willing to contribute to a project, leaving our job for a new one, or even starting a new business. Commitment can also pertain to more personal aspects of life, such as getting married, buying a home, exercise, our prayer lives, eating better, or dropping bad habits.

When I launched Serviam Partners, I had to overcome my own risk aversion to be fully committed and "burn my ships." I could not fail as my family was depending on me, so I put everything I had into ensuring my business would be successful. *There was no going back.* The same is true of the Leadership Foundry (www.MyLeadershipFoundry.com), which I co-founded with Brandon Smith in 2018. We started small and carefully refined our model, feeling confident it would be successful. After lots of committed effort, we are thrilled that this fast-growing business we love continues to thrive.

As much as I believe in the power of full commitment, I also recognize that good contingency planning and cultivating multiple options is also prudent in business and life. This might apply to most of the decisions we make on any given day. But, as I hope you will agree, there are going to be critical moments in our lives where we need to be 100 percent committed and hold nothing back. The ships may have to be burned in these critical moments, and we can't hedge our bets.

What Gets in the Way?

I believe there is one primary obstacle (that surpasses all other obstacles). That obstacle is a *thought*—the thought that if things don't work out, we will always have an escape plan to fall back on. Knowing we have an escape plan prevents us from giving every ounce of effort needed for true success, achieving difficult goals, or making meaningful changes in our lives.

Here are **four ways** to grow our commitment muscles and more readily embrace our "Veracruz moments":

1. **Get accountability partners.** They can help keep you on track, challenge you, and encourage you. Find someone who will not let you off the hook for giving less than a total effort and full commitment to whatever you are trying to do.

2. **Don't struggle in silence.** If faced with "Veracruz moments," ask for help. Get advice from trusted friends and mentors. Do your homework. Don't face these big decisions alone. Chances are, someone you know has been through something similar in their own life and can offer invaluable insights and perspectives.

3. **Make bold public goals.** I have often found this to be a useful mind trick to help me accomplish big goals or projects. Here is an example: When I am writing a series of blog posts, I share the title of the next post that will come out the following week. Most of the time, this new post is not yet written, and I am highly motivated to write it to honor my weekly public announcement (commitment). It's a simple trick, but it works for me.

4. **Be clear about the worthiness of the outcome you seek.** Having a clear understanding of the worthiness of the outcomes you desire in any area of your life can often properly motivate you to be all in. For example, you may be nervous about taking ownership of a new project at work, but you know the project will fail unless you lead it.

If you agree that being all in at the appropriate times is important, what are the fruits of this total commitment? Here are **three positive outcomes** I have observed in the lives of others and in my own experience:

1. **Clarity of purpose.** You are single-minded about your goal(s) and fully aware of *why* you are making the effort. Also, the hoped-for outcome and the hard work connected to your commitment level exist in relative harmony.
2. **Focused, efficient, and effective**. When you are all in, you are able to more efficiently apply your energy and resources toward a single effort versus hedging your bets on multiple efforts.
3. **The fastest path to success**. You will obviously reach your goal faster if you give it all you've got and not hedge your bets, but this can also be scary. Take a moment and ask yourself: Does the success I hope to attain or goal I want to achieve outweigh my fear of the commitment level necessary to get there?" This will bring you to the "Veracruz moment" of decision.

Perhaps you are faced with "Veracruz moments" right now and are unsure of what to do. Many of us may delay important decisions, put off pursuing our dreams, or avoid risk out of caution, raw fear, or some other reason. Maybe it's time to face these critical moments and abandon your escape plan. Carefully consider whether you are ready to go all in regarding a big decision in your life and be 100 percent committed.

It may be time to burn the ships.

Are you facing a big decision in your life at this time?
What can you do to be "all in" and move forward?

CHAPTER 20

Mentoring the Next Generation

While I made my living as a coach, I have lived my life to be a mentor—and to be mentored!—constantly. Everything in the world has been passed down. Every piece of knowledge is something that has been shared by someone else. If you understand it as I do, mentoring becomes your true legacy. It is the greatest inheritance you can give to others. It is why you get up every day—to teach and be taught.

JOHN WOODEN, LEGENDARY UCLA BASKETBALL COACH AND
AUTHOR OF *A GAME PLAN FOR LIFE*

Not long ago, over the span of a few weeks I encountered four young adults ranging in age from nineteen to twenty-six. They made such a favorable impression on me that I feel compelled to share the experiences in this book. I was struck by the consistent, positive behaviors they all exhibited, despite their diverse backgrounds and the various reasons they had for wanting to speak with me. Each of them demonstrated sincere *courtesy, curiosity,* and *gratitude,* and they all *followed up* with me in a timely manner based on the different subjects we had discussed. As an added bonus, each of them sent me a handwritten thank-you note. Why do these behaviors stand out? In today's world, I am likely to observe one, possibly two at most, of these behaviors I value so highly from people of *any* age, but rarely do I encounter all four behaviors at once. To say the least, I was intrigued and wanted to understand what made these four young adults different.

I reached out to each of them to specifically ask where they had learned these behaviors and who had taught them. Again, there was remarkable consistency from these four very different young adults as they answered my questions. Each of them described the positive influence of their parents growing up and later the influence of helpful mentors in college. The three who were out of college and in the workplace described a caring boss or senior-level mentor who had taken them under their wing and taught (and modeled) the value of courtesy, curiosity, gratitude, and follow up. I suspected this would be the case, but it was affirming to hear it straight from these remarkable young people.

Why Does This Matter?

I am truly grateful to have had the opportunity to frequently speak on college campuses and mentor young professionals over the last two decades. I have heard for years the criticism leveled at this emerging generation of future leaders by older professionals who bemoan what they perceive to be a lack of interest in practicing the positive behaviors I shared in this chapter. At times I have been critical as well. Maybe, though, if the lessons from these four young adults means anything, we should point the finger of blame at ourselves and not them. *Maybe the students were ready all along and the teachers were nowhere to be found . . .*

Those of us who are parents have a wonderful opportunity to teach our children the lessons and values that will make them successful in life and in the professional world. Do we make the most of this opportunity and the short amount of time we have them under our roofs to achieve this goal? For those of us who are leaders, do we look at our younger colleagues with a jaundiced eye and level unfair criticism at them, or do we embrace our clear responsibility to teach them what we have learned and prepare them to lead? Do we actively give time to students in the schools we attended or in the communities where we live? How many younger colleagues at work are we mentoring right now? How much time do we invest in sharing lessons and stories from our career with junior members of our company, illuminating the keys to our success and helping them learn from our failures? By the way, I would suggest that we not wait for the perfect company program to act, but instead treat mentorship as the urgent and ongoing responsibility of every leader.

I hope as you read this chapter, you will not feel offended but rather *encouraged* and *inspired* to be the positive mentor that young adults will identify one day in the future as someone who helped, guided, taught, and coached them to success. I know my younger son has benefited tremendously from the generous mentors who have helped influence his life. With the demands of family, business, and other commitments, I know I sometimes fall short in this area, and you may be feeling the same. Regardless, I know most of us can do better. Surely we can find time to invest in the future. Even if we start with mentoring just one young adult after reading this book, that will be a start. Don't let uncertainty or self-doubt get in the way: I believe *everyone* has something of value to share with others.

If you are already an encouraging and helpful mentor to the next generation of leaders, then I would like to share my sincere gratitude. If you have gifts, wisdom, and lessons to share and are willing to find time to share them, please take on this challenge without delay. Finally, I have a surprise to share that good mentors already know: as we spend time mentoring younger colleagues, *they typically inspire and teach us valuable lessons as well.*

*What valuable insights from your life and experiences
can you share with an aspiring leader today?
Be open to what they can teach you as well.*

CHAPTER 21

Are You Successful?

Try not to become a man of success. Rather become a man of value.
ALBERT EINSTEIN

My father typically comes to our house for a visit two or three times a year. He loves to see his grandsons, and we talk to him every week by phone, but because of his health it is sometimes difficult for him to travel from his Florida home to Atlanta. One particular weekend visit was different, however, because of a powerful lesson he helped me teach one of my children. On the Saturday afternoon of my dad's visit several years ago, my younger son and I were throwing the football outside while my father was taking a short nap in his room. I can always tell when one of my boys has something on his mind, so I probed and asked my son if there was anything he wanted to talk about. He responded with, "Dad, remember when we talked about what it means to be successful a few months ago? Were Nana and Papa successful?"

Wow! That was an interesting and mature question. He was referring to a conversation we had a few months before about being successful in business and what kind of career he wanted to have after college. I gave him a thoroughly modern version of what I thought success looked like in business and made sure we talked about having strong faith and the importance of starting and caring for a family someday as well. I kept it at a high level for him at that time, but his question about my parents deserved a deeper answer.

I explained that my mom and dad came from a different generation. He was in the army for six years after high school before going to work full-time. He met and married my mother, who also worked for the same company, in 1965, and I came along in 1966. We didn't have a lot of extras when I was growing up, but we had what we needed. Both my parents worked, but we always had dinner together, and my father frequently coached my sports teams. They were both active volunteers at our church and volunteered in the community where we lived. Even though my parents did not finish college, they both instilled in me a passion for learning when I was young, and there was no question in their minds that I would continue my education after high school. The same was true for my younger sister.

My parents taught us about faith, the importance of serving others, and the value of hard work. My sister and I knew how to be self-sufficient at a young age. Strong values and great life lessons were instilled in us from early childhood. My parents also handled adversity in their lives with a calmness and determination that inspires me to this day. So, were my parents successful? By modern standards, a quick glance at their meager savings and lack of material possessions would merit a resounding "no." But in the areas that mattered most to my father—and to my mother while she was alive—my parents were incredibly blessed all their lives with everything of consequence they truly desired.

You see, my parents never tried to "keep up with the Joneses." Acquiring toys and accumulating wealth never mattered. They were focused on raising faith-filled children, helping as much as possible with furthering our education, and teaching us how to be responsible. These days my father always wants to talk about his grandchildren or find out how my business is doing when I call him. He rarely talks about himself, and he certainly never complains.

My parents came from a generation that has much to teach us. We can deceive ourselves all we want that today's world holds us to a different standard, but as I get older, I recognize that we also have the ability to choose the lives we want to lead. The more I detach myself from modern society's view of success, the happier and more fulfilled I feel. This detachment allows me to put the appropriate focus on serving God and living my faith, loving and spending time with my wife and children, and giving back to others instead of accumulating unnecessary toys that can often become obstacles to true happiness. I learned these invaluable lessons from my parents—especially my father.

So, back to my son's question: "Were Nana and Papa successful?" As I reflect on their lives and write this chapter, I have to say that my parents were the most successful people I have ever known. I hope I can emulate their example over the course of my life.

The idea of success that many of us have been taught at a young age is often an illusion that can create frustration, anxiety, and years of wasted time as we wind up chasing things that may not be what we need or even important as we grow older. My parents were wise enough to avoid this trap, and did their best to convey the lesson to me, although I must admit I spent the early years of my career desperately trying to live up to the expectations the world placed before me.

My father, who is now in his eighties, has spent most of his life disinterested in anything other than becoming the best husband, father, grandfather, and selfless servant to others that he can be. He has never chased the illusion of worldly success that drives so many others, and yet he is the happiest and most fulfilled man I know. My mother had the exact same approach to life until her death in 2009.

This topic may seem like an odd one to include in this book, but isn't having clarity about *why* we do what we do and our goals in life incredibly fundamental and important? Reflect on what it is you are chasing in life and carefully consider whether you are fulfilled. This is a question we all must answer for ourselves.

After pondering the lessons of this chapter, how will you know if you have been successful? Is your current definition of success truly making you happy? If not, work at developing a new one that may draw on the lessons from my parents that I have shared.

CHAPTER 22

The Mosaic of Your Life

At the end it's not about what you have or even what you've accomplished. It's about who you've lifted up, who you've made better . . . what you've given back.

DENZEL WASHINGTON

When we think of a mosaic, we usually think of tiles of glass or stone that have been formed into a beautiful image by an artist. I was reflecting recently about the wonderful "mosaic" my dad has created in his long life as a father, husband, friend, and servant of his community. The "tiles" of his life are represented by the countless acts of kindness he has performed, the sacrifices he has always made for his family, and the lifetime of service he has rendered his church and community. It is obvious to all who know him that selfless love and a generous spirit are at the heart of all these deeds. Like all of us, he has made mistakes along the way, but the mosaic of his life is something beautiful to reflect on and aspire to emulate. I think of the exemplary life of my dear departed mother in much the same way. I bet you have similar role models in your own life.

Thoughtfully consider what kind of life mosaic you will

create today, this week, this year, and over the course of your life. Will it be a beautiful work of art or something you will be ashamed for others to see? The tiles of your mosaic are made up of the interactions you have with others, how you care for your family and loved ones, the relationships you build, the work you produce, the strength of your faith, and the service you render to your community. The opportunities to make a difference and the decision points you have each day are almost endless. In these important moments, how will you show up? How will you act? Will the thought that you have the opportunity to create something special and beautiful cross your mind?

The quality of tiles we contribute to our own mosaics will be dramatically affected by the love, selflessness, generosity, kindness, and gratitude we apply to their creation. My wish for all of us is that we will use the imagery of the life mosaic to be more intentional and thoughtful about how we show up and act today and every day. Fifty years from now I hope the picture we each will have assembled is beautiful, breathtaking, and inspiring to others—and not something stashed in the basement like an unwanted Christmas gift.

When my dad reads this chapter, I know he will say that he is not finished creating the mosaic of his life, and he is correct. He will also say that you must be patient and do the best you can every day to make progress toward a more meaningful life. I hope this artist who is my father will keep on inspiring me and those who know him for years to come as he finishes his masterpiece. I hope to follow in his footsteps in some small way and inspire my children and future grandchildren to do the same.

What will the mosaic of your life look like someday?

Conclusion

Reflections from My Morning Walks to Draper Lake

We make a living by what we get; we make a life by what we give.
WINSTON CHURCHILL

In the days leading up to pulling the final version of this book together, my family and I enjoyed a much-needed vacation in Blue Mountain Beach, located on Florida's Gulf Coast. There was a beautiful lake a few miles from our condo where I would walk each morning just after sunrise before my family woke up. During these solitary walks, I did a lot of reflecting, praying, and thinking about this book. It dawned on me during my third morning walk to Draper Lake that this book is a gift I have been wanting to share with others for years. It represents most of the topics I care about and coach others on in my professional life. I always tell my coaching clients that my main goal is to help them visualize what professional and personal "success" looks like for them and then work at identifying and removing the obstacles to achieving that success. This book, with its various and eclectic topics, is an effort to give students, wisdom seekers, established leaders, and aspiring leaders a guidebook to grow in all the areas that matter most . . . and hopefully remove the obstacles that have been standing in their way.

This reflection time each morning also reminded me that I have been incredibly fortunate over the course of my time on this earth to receive many gifts that have made a tremendous difference in every aspect of my life. I am not talking about a new car, a new watch, or a new shirt for Christmas. I am talking about the thoughtful gifts from family, friends, and even relative strangers that have changed my thinking, inspired me, taught me valuable lessons, and gotten me back on track when I was lost.

Let me share **six invaluable gifts** that really stand out in my memory:

1. **The gift of wisdom** from my parents over the course of my life. This gift was often subtle and exactly what I needed at the time, even though at times I was resistant and unwilling to listen. This wisdom has echoed through the generations as I find myself sharing my parents' lessons with my own children.

2. **The gift of inspiration** from my oldest son Alex, who has high-functioning autism. His joyful willingness to engage with a world each day that is often hostile and alien to people on the autism spectrum inspires me and everyone who knows him.

3. **The gift of allowing others to help me** from my good friend Jim. He cared enough about me over a decade ago

to help me understand that although I enjoyed helping others, I often struggled to let others help me. His advice was a game-changer that taught me to gratefully receive the help that I so enjoy giving to others.

4. **A thoughtful challenge** from my dear friend Ron. He gave me a beautiful leather journal in 2001 and challenged me to write down my thoughts and share them with others. I have since filled up more than twenty leather journals, and my writing has translated into hundreds of articles and eight published books, the last of which is the one you are reading now.

5. **The gift of encouragement** from so many friends who urged me to start my own company in 2013. Their willingness to push me out of my comfort zone to do work I love as a solopreneur was the spark that gave me the courage to launch Serviam Partners.

6. **The gift of self-reflection** from my wife, who helped me recognize the need to slow down the hectic place of my life many years ago. Through reflection, I've been able to be more fully present for my loved ones, friends, and causes I care about, and this has been an invaluable gift.

I could name dozens of invaluable gifts that have had a meaningful impact on my life. If we slow down enough to appreciate and be present in the encounters we have with others each day, we will begin to realize an endless stream of gifts and recognize the difference these gifts are making in our lives. Once we become aware of the value and power of what we receive from others, we can more intentionally share our own gifts through candid advice for a co-worker, sharing a helpful book, lending a listening ear for a troubled friend, coaching a younger colleague, sharing a little hard-fought wisdom with our children, and more.

Mastering the concept of gifts will make your life and the lives of everyone around you richer and more rewarding. As you reflect on the life-changing gifts you have received from others, r*each out and thank the givers.* Consider how you can pass along your own gifts in a more intentional way through the daily interactions you will have with others—*and never expect anything in return.*

This book is my gift to you, and I hope you have found it helpful.

Now that you have read Essential Wisdom *and the lessons it contains, how will you better share your gifts with others?*

Acknowledgments

At the conclusion of each of my books, I find myself sincerely thanking an eclectic "village" of family, friends, and collaborators who help bring my work to life. First and foremost, I thank God for the privilege to do work I love each and every day, and I pray it will be for his honor and glory, not mine. I wish to thank my wonderful wife, Sandra. She is my rock, and I am truly grateful for her unwavering love and support over the years. I am grateful to my sons, Alex and Ryan, for their support and being part of the motivation to write this book. I am truly thankful to be their dad.

Thank you to my Leadership Foundry co-founder, Brandon, for your friendship, partnership, and wise counsel over the years. Chester, Pat, and Tim are friends, best-selling authors, leadership experts, and world-class human beings who have taught me a great deal about life and leadership . . . thank you!

I appreciate the assistance of Lauren Ashe who helped me pull together an early version of this manuscript. I look forward to reading the books you will write in the years ahead! Thank you to my editor Claudia Volkman for your assistance and expertise in shaping the final version of *Essential Wisdom* and for never failing to challenge me to do my best. I am grateful to Karen Daniel for your partnership, friendship, and book cover design for this book and for all the work we have done together over the years. Thank you to Lisa Guthrie for the invaluable proofreading work you did in the final stages of the book. I appreciate your keen eye!

To all who reviewed the book, offered suggestions, and gave recommendations, please know I truly appreciate your help and support. Thank you to my WBC men's group for your friendship, support, and for always challenging me to show up well as a father, husband, leader, and Catholic man.

Ron, thank you for the beautiful leather journal you gave me in 2001 with the challenge to share my thoughts with others and become a writer. As I complete this, my eighth book, I think back on your encouragement and friendship with sincere gratitude. Thank you, my friend.

Mom, thank you for your love, encouragement, and wisdom. You are sorely missed, and I hope to see you again in Heaven. Dad, thank you for the wise counsel you never cease to give and the incredible testimony of your life. I am grateful you are my father.

About the Author

Randy Hain is the founder and president of Serviam Partners (ServiamPartners.com) and the co-founder of the Leadership Foundry (MyLeadershipFoundry.com). With a successful twenty-five-plus-year career in senior leadership roles, corporate talent, and executive search, he is a sought-after executive coach for senior leaders at some of the best-known companies in the U.S. who are seeking expert guidance on identifying and overcoming obstacles to their success or developing new leadership skills. He is also an expert at onboarding and cultural assimilation for senior leaders as well as helping senior leadership teams improve trust, clarity, collaboration, and candid communication. Randy also offers consulting and coaching for companies, teams, and individual business leaders looking to develop more authentic and effective business relationships both inside and outside their organizations. His deep expertise in business relationships is a true area of differentiation for him and Serviam Partners.

He is an active community leader and serves on the

board of Growing Leaders (www.GrowingLeaders.com). As a member of the Advisory Board for the Brock School of Business at Samford University, Randy frequently presents on relevant business topics to the students there. He is passionate about promoting autism awareness and advocating for adults with autism in the workplace. He also leads the Faith@Work ministry at St. Peter Chanel Catholic Church. Randy has earned a reputation as a creative business partner and generous thought leader through his books, articles, and speaking engagements.

Randy is the award-winning author of seven other books, including *Something More: The Professional's Pursuit of a Meaningful Life, LANDED! Proven Job Search Strategies for Today's Professional,* and *Special Children, Blessed Fathers: Encouragement for Fathers of Children with Special Needs,* all available on Amazon.

Learn more about Randy Hain's professional work, books, blog posts, and thought leadership at his website, www.ServiamPartners.com.

Made in the USA
Columbia, SC
04 October 2021

46673462R10093